Instructional Feedback

To all the great teachers in our lives.

Instructional Feedback

The Power, the Promise, the Practice

Jeffrey K. Smith

Anastasiya A. Lipnevich

Thomas R. Guskey

Foreword by Rick Stiggins

FOR INFORMATION:

Corwin
A SAGE Company
2455 Teller Road
Thousand Oaks, California 91320
(800) 233-9936
www.corwin.com

SAGE Publications Ltd.
1 Oliver's Yard
55 City Road
London EC1Y 1SP
United Kingdom

SAGE Publications India Pvt. Ltd.
Unit No 323-333, Third Floor, F-Block
International Trade Tower Nehru Place
New Delhi 110 019
India

SAGE Publications Asia-Pacific Pte. Ltd.
18 Cross Street #10-10/11/12
China Square Central
Singapore 048423

President: Mike Soules
Vice President and
  Editorial Director: Monica Eckman
Publisher: Jessica Allan
Content Development Editor: Mia Rodriguez
Production Editor: Tori Mirsadjadi
Copy Editor: Melinda Masson
Typesetter: C&M Digitals (P) Ltd.
Cover Designer: Candice Harman
Marketing Manager: Olivia Bartlett

Paperback ISBN 978-1-5443-8521-1

This book is printed on acid-free paper.

23 24 25 26 27 10 9 8 7 6 5 4 3 2 1

CONTENTS

Note From the Publisher: The authors have provided video and web content throughout the book that is available to you through QR (quick response) codes. To read a QR code, you must have a smartphone or tablet with a camera. We recommend that you download a QR code reader app that is made specifically for your phone or tablet brand.

FOREWORD

The spirit of this book and of its three authors is captured in the following sentence from Chapter 1: "We want to help you to provide the kind of feedback to your students that will foster their academic growth, build their sense of self-efficacy, and help them to critically evaluate their progress as learners." It has been a tradition to think of feedback as focusing on students' cognitive (learning) development, and, to be sure, this is central to the teachings of Smith, Lipnevich, and Guskey. But most exciting for me is the fact that they don't stop there—far from it. They turn the spotlight with equal brilliance on the emotional dynamics of teaching and learning from the student's perspective.

On the academic side, the metaphor that I believe best characterizes these authors' vision of the role of feedback in promoting learning success is that of GPS navigation—in fact, the authors refer to this notion. Give students a destination port (their learning target), map a pathway for them to their port with signposts along the way, and use feedback to guide them from posts to port to successfully complete their journey. All the information student sailors need to track their own progress, remain confident as they travel, and arrive with all flags flying is made readily available to them through ongoing descriptive feedback. There are no surprises along the way, and, if difficulties arise, the students know what to do about it.

An exciting dimension of this book is that the authors delve into what happens within the emotions and thinking of learners as they leave port on their journey and travel. It isn't merely that they learn more. Done well and used effectively, feedback can also keep learners believing in themselves. The authors label these emotional dynamics "academic self-efficacy" and "self-evaluation." They grant these ideas careful attention because of their potential contributions to student academic success. They are foundational to all students becoming the confident lifelong learners they absolutely must be as they mature in these dynamically changing times. Let me explain why.

Psychologist and Stanford professor Albert Bandura (1994) provides us with a practical way to understand self-efficacy and see why it must be regarded as an essential outcome of the schooling process. He teaches this lesson by defining the concept in terms of anchor points on a continuum:

The strong end:

A strong sense of efficacy enhances human accomplishment and personal well-being in many ways. People with high assurance in their capabilities approach difficult tasks as challenges to be mastered rather than as threats to be avoided. Such an efficacious outlook fosters intrinsic interest and deep engrossment in activities. They set themselves challenging goals and maintain strong commitment to them. They heighten and sustain their efforts in the face of failure. They quickly recover their sense of efficacy after failures or setbacks. They attribute failure to insufficient effort or deficient knowledge and skills which are acquirable. They approach threatening situations with assurance that they can exercise control over them. Such an efficacious outlook produces personal accomplishments, reduces stress and lowers vulnerability. . . .

The weak end:

In contrast, people who doubt their capabilities shy away from difficult tasks which they view as personal threats. They have low aspirations and weak commitment to the goals they choose to pursue. When faced with difficult tasks, they dwell on their personal deficiencies, on the obstacles they will encounter, and all kinds of adverse outcomes rather than concentrate on how to perform successfully. They slacken their efforts and give up quickly in the face of difficulties. They are slow to recover their sense of efficacy following failure or setbacks. Because they view insufficient performance as deficient aptitude it does not require much failure for them to lose faith in their capabilities. (p. 71)

Our mission as teachers is to move as many of our students as we can as close to the positive end of this continuum as we can. The role of feedback as defined in this book is to provide the motor and the motivation needed to get students there by working with us, their teachers, to manage their own success. The power and value of feedback increase as students' sense of academic self-efficacy strengthens. Learners become increasingly confident in their ability to control their own success. On the other hand, feedback is of lesser value at the low end of the Bandura continuum, because students may not understand it, know what to do about it, or feel empowered to act on it. They will remain powerless to control their own success. In order for students to become increasingly efficacious, they must experience ongoing success in their learning. Feedback is the motor that can power that ongoing success.

This is precisely why the ideas and strategies offered by Smith, Lipnevich, and Guskey, our teachers, are so crucial to our practical understanding of feedback as a teaching and learning tool. They reach into the history of thinking about effective feedback to connect us with the insightful thinking, for example, of Royce Sadler, who instructs us that assessment and feedback can have maximum impact when we use them to keep students constantly informed about where they are headed in their learning, where they are now, and how they can close the gap between the two. The locus of control over their unfolding success must remain with the learners.

Our teachers in this book instruct us that the power of instructional feedback is tapped when we center it on the learning, describing for students how to do better the next time as they work through the progressions of increasing competence. This comprehensive analysis of the best current thinking about instructional feedback leads us to one final mission: Leave the students ready, willing, and able to act in the service of their ongoing learning success. This is the foundation for confident lifelong learning.

Rick Stiggins
Portland, OR

PREFACE

Teaching is a wondrous and wonderful blend of art and science. It is a craft consisting of equal parts heart and brain. We have often heard it said, "Teachers are born, not made." Perhaps, but one could also say that of ballerinas, and they receive extensive training before they take the stage.

As researchers, we sit for the most part on the science side of the educational enterprise. We teach as well, of course, and we are duly proud of awards that we have won for our teaching. But in this endeavor, our goal is to take the science that has accumulated in recent years concerning the impact of instructional feedback and refine it for use in real classrooms: yours.

Our goal in *Instructional Feedback: The Power, the Promise, the Practice* is to present you with a distilled version of what the research says about providing feedback in a fashion that will be most useful for you and your students. Thus, we present references where we think they are warranted and where we think you might want to look at the citations listed, but not so many that they clog up the flow of the text. Additionally, having worked with thousands of teachers over the years, we know that although we have some good ideas for the classroom application of the concepts we present, you will likely have more and, perhaps, better ones—certainly better for your circumstances. So we offer these ideas primarily for your reflection.

Finally, we know that for most teachers, if they could have a 48-hour day, they'd spend 40 of those hours thinking about how to better help their kids. So, in this book, we tried to look for ways in which you can be both efficient and effective in providing feedback. We also tried to make reading *Instructional Feedback: The Power, the Promise, the Practice* a pleasant and perhaps even enjoyable activity.

Jeffrey, Anastasiya, and Thomas

ABOUT THE AUTHORS

Jeffrey K. Smith is a professor and formerly the dean of the College of Education at the University of Otago in New Zealand. He earned his bachelor's degree from Princeton and his PhD from the University of Chicago. He taught at Rutgers University in New Jersey for 29 years where he was the chair of the Educational Psychology Department. He moved to New Zealand in 2005 and has been there ever since. While teaching at Rutgers, Dr. Smith served as a consultant to the Metropolitan Museum of Art, where he was the head of the Office of Research and Evaluation. He has written over 100 research articles and 10 books on assessment and the psychology of aesthetics, including being co-editor of *The Cambridge Handbook of Instructional Feedback.*

Anastasiya A. Lipnevich is a professor of educational psychology at Queens College and the Graduate Center of the City University of New York. Originally from Belarus, Dr. Lipnevich received her combined master's degree in clinical psychology, education, and Italian language from the Belarusian State Pedagogical University, followed by her master's in counseling psychology from Rutgers University. She then earned her PhD in educational psychology (learning, cognition, and development concentration), also from Rutgers University. She co-edited two books—*Psychosocial Skills and School Systems in the 21st Century* (Lipnevich, Preckel, & Roberts, 2016; Springer) and *The Cambridge Handbook of Instructional Feedback* (Lipnevich & Smith, 2018; Cambridge University Press)—and numerous articles. She may be contacted at www.anastasiyalipnevich.com or a.lipnevich@gmail.com.

Thomas R. Guskey is professor emeritus in the College of Education at the University of Kentucky. A graduate of the University of Chicago, he began his career in education as a middle school teacher, served as a school administrator in Chicago Public Schools, and was the first director of the Center for the Improvement of Teaching and Learning, a national educational research center. He is a Fellow in the American Educational Research Association and was awarded the Association's prestigious *Relating Research to Practice Award*. Dr. Guskey is the author or editor of 25 award-winning books and more than 300 book chapters and articles. His most recent books include *Implementing Mastery Learning* (2023), *Get Set, Go! Creating Successful Grading and Reporting Systems* (2020), *What We Know About Grading* (with Brookhart, 2019), and *On Your Mark: Challenging the Conventions of Grading and Reporting* (2015). He may be contacted by email at guskey@uky.edu, on Twitter at @tguskey, or at www.tguskey.com.

INTRODUCTION

What Is Instructional Feedback All About?

A theory in physics states that there are an infinite number of universes, and we simply inhabit one of them. So imagine that for Kiya Reilly, a fifth-grade student who is awaiting the receipt of the essay she handed in last Friday, the universe splits into six different realities as Ms. MacLemore gives back her essay. In these different universes, Kiya receives the following feedback:

Universe 1	Universe 2	Universe 3
Kiya, what an interesting story! You really got my attention and held it. Let's work on a couple of things before we move on to publishing it. In particular, let's look at how you are presenting dialog . . .	*The story is good here, but your dialog isn't how people really talk to one another. Do you talk to your friends that way? See if you can sharpen that up.*	*You're such a good writer! Keep up the great work!*
What Really Happened at the Mall **Kiya Reilly** **I didn't really think about it. Maybe I should have. But when I saw Mom standing in the checkout with that ugly . . .**	**What Really Happened at the Mall** **Kiya Reilly** **I didn't really think about it. Maybe I should have. But when I saw Mom standing in the checkout with that ugly . . .**	**What Really Happened at the Mall** **Kiya Reilly** **I didn't really think about it. Maybe I should have. But when I saw Mom standing in the checkout with that ugly . . .**

Universe 4	Universe 5	Universe 6
There are a lot of errors here. See if you can spot some of them on your own.	*This is one of the better papers handed in on this assignment, but there is a ways to go on it.*	*√+*
What Really Happened at the Mall **Kiya Reilly** **I didn't really think about it. Maybe I should have. But when I saw Mom standing in the checkout with that ugly . . .**	**What Really Happened at the Mall** **Kiya Reilly** **I didn't really think about it. Maybe I should have. But when I saw Mom standing in the checkout with that ugly . . .**	**What Really Happened at the Mall** **Kiya Reilly** **I didn't really think about it. Maybe I should have. But when I saw Mom standing in the checkout with that ugly . . .**

In which universe does Kiya eagerly engage in improving this particular essay and think about how she can make first drafts of future work stronger? Which universe would you choose to live in?

Imagine you are Kiya receiving these different feedback messages. The differences may seem subtle, but if you read each of them carefully and then check your reactions to them, in terms of both how you feel and what you might do on a revision, you might find the differences are real and important:

- Feedback 1 addresses you directly. This seems like a discussion between people who have a history and like one another. It also seems to say that Ms. MacLemore and you are in this together. It is very engaging, encourages more work on the story, and suggests that there is a positive goal to work toward, as well as that others will read this work.

- Feedback 2 has a nice comment on the story overall, but the rest of that comment might be taken one of two ways: as a rather harsh criticism (are you that oblivious to how you and your friends talk?) or as a suggestion on how to improve (think about how you really talk and then go with that in your dialog).

- Feedback 3 might be very encouraging and cause you to think that writing really is your strong area, but then you don't do so well in math. What does that mean?

- Feedback 4 just focuses on the negative. Did Ms. MacLemore like the story at all? Why didn't she comment on what you actually wrote rather than what you got wrong? It does encourage you to search for errors and thus engage in active processing, but are you ready to do it on your own?

- Feedback 5 simply compares you to others, and says to work more. On what? Go where? How about some advice?

- Feedback 6 might engender a "So what?" reaction, but if you had worked hard on this story, it might cause you to wonder why you put so much effort in, and cause you to back off some on your next piece.

For us as teachers, the success of our instructional efforts is defined by the success of our students. Their achievement is our achievement. They are the vehicle through which our efforts are realized. One of the most important ways we reach our students is through the feedback we provide on their work.

One of the most important ways we reach our students is through the feedback we provide on their work.

For a high school English teacher with 100 students in four or five classes, written feedback on assignments (as opposed to oral feedback) may be the most important form of communication with students. For a primary teacher with 25 children in the class, feedback can be a source of encouragement, reflection, and the development of self-efficacy. It can also communicate that the teacher is really listening and cares about what each student is doing. For example, for a music teacher working one-on-one with students, feedback may represent a constant dialog with countless loops per lesson.

Feedback in a music lesson is a constant dialog.

As much as feedback can encourage, support, and inspire, feedback that is given thoughtlessly or harshly can engender anxiety, fear, or a loss of self-efficacy.

Feedback that is given thoughtlessly or harshly can engender anxiety, fear, or a loss of self-efficacy.

Seeing "This is rubbish!" on your work could cause you to avoid similar tasks and engender a slew of negative emotions. Despite the fact that scholars may still argue over the strength of feedback's effect on student performance, learning, and personality, we know that certain types of feedback can define students' lives.

In life, we receive feedback in all sorts of situations, ranging from medical tests, to interpersonal interactions, to baking a cake. Sometimes we eagerly anticipate that feedback, and other times we dread it. Have you ever wondered what causes that eagerness or fear? What does good feedback look like, and what does it do? What makes feedback effective—and effective for what? Are there any universal rules for providing or receiving feedback, or do the rules vary by context and by situation?

Our goal in this book is simple: We want to help you to provide the kind of feedback to your students that will foster their academic growth, build their sense of self-efficacy, and help them to critically evaluate their progress as learners. We won't provide a prescription for offering feedback simply because we are all different and each learning situation is different. What we will provide is an approach to thinking about feedback, maybe better described as a lens for looking at how to provide feedback, in order to maximize its usefulness to students and to build a better learning relationship with students. We will also discuss instructional supports that teachers can implement to encourage students to engage in self-feedback. After all, we want students to grow and develop into autonomous learners who can generate their own feedback based on the information they receive from teachers, peers, or the task itself. We also hope to have some fun along the way and to provide a wealth of practical examples for you to take back to your classroom.

A POINT OF VIEW

Although we don't want to burden you with a philosophy of education, allow us to give you what we might call "a point of view." We believe that you are concerned about your students: their educational growth, their development as individuals, their interactions with others, and their happiness. We are also concerned about you: your professional development, your work–life balance, your relationship with family and friends, and *your* happiness. So in this book, we do our best to provide you with practical, *usable* advice about how to provide feedback that not only is student-centered, based on solid evidence, and effective, but also respects your time and resources.

As teachers, we tend to think of feedback as the comments we make on a student's essay or a mathematics test. We look for mistakes and provide either a correct answer or a better alternative. We then put a grade at the top of the paper and move on. Research shows us that this is a relatively ineffective approach if our goal is to facilitate learning, increase performance, or improve students' approaches and strategies of learning.

We propose a different point of view on feedback. Instead of viewing it as basically corrective and grade-oriented, what if we consider feedback as another form of instruction? What if we weren't solely interested in student learning and growth, but also cared a great deal about their emotional well-being? And what if we acknowledged that we are working with students toward a shared goal? Instead of pointing out errors and comparing students to their classmates, we could say things like "I really like the way you organized your presentation! I felt that some graphs needed more information, so let's focus on these for your next talk." This example feedback message attends to emotion, provides advice on how to improve rather than focusing on what was wrong, and, most importantly, offers another try.

This is precisely the perspective we present in this book. How can we look at students as if they were our partners in learning? How would that change our behavior? And how can we do that with 25 children in a fifth-grade class, or 100 students in first-year high school English? Admittedly, it's a challenge. But we have some great ideas that we think will help.

What if we thought of our students as our partners in learning?

Source: istock.com/xavierarnau

Let's get started.

EXEMPLARY EXEMPLAR: *LA MAESTRA*

One of your authors and his wife were watching a cooking class in Tuscany, where a dozen tourists were learning how to make ravioli of different colors. Eleven students were succeeding nicely and having a great time, but one lady at the end of the long table had a green pesto pasta that looked like soup. She was clearly distraught, and her husband was teasing her. The instructor noticed the interaction and went to address the potential disaster. We had been admiring the quality of the instructor's teaching and enthusiasm, and asked each other, "How is she going to handle this?" Her student was close to bursting out in tears.

The instructor glided past the other students and when she came upon the green ooze exclaimed, "This is *beautiful*! Now, we make it *perfect*!" The woman absolutely beamed, and the instructor went on to tell the whole group, "When we have the color beautiful like this, we just add more flour, and the pasta is complete." The key here is that the instructor recognized the emotional component of the situation, defused it, and then was prepared to provide feedback. She used it as a teachable moment to all, thus sparing any sense of failure for the one student and allowing all students to nod in appreciation of this important feedback. A masterful move.

(Continued)

(Continued)

Feedback is important in all forms of teaching!

Source: istock.com/xavierarnau

WHAT IS THE PROMISE OF FEEDBACK?

We chose to include *Promise* in the subtitle for this book because we believe feedback is one of the most important and influential aspects of teaching. Feedback points out mistakes and celebrates successes, encourages additional effort, convinces students that they can succeed, makes suggestions on more productive routes of working, gives students new ways of thinking about their work, and offers students the opportunity to take another shot at what they are doing. You do that normally in your everyday teaching. But you can bring that same perspective to providing feedback as well. You can think of it like this: *Feedback is teaching based on current information.*

Feedback is teaching based on current information.

That teaching can consist of information provided to the class as a whole, especially when you see many students having the same difficulty or ready for the same extended idea, or to individuals when you see particular needs or opportunities. More than anything else, powerful feedback *helps*. Therefore, the most important question we need to ask ourselves with every form of feedback should be "Is this helping?"

The most helpful type of feedback must be used by students.

Studies on feedback show that it isn't always effective and can, under certain conditions, actually be harmful! But this research also shows that when used properly, feedback can be one of the most powerful instructional tools available to teachers. To realize that power, however, feedback must be received by learners, clearly understood, and acted upon. Just like the most perfectly delivered lecture must be processed by students to be effective, the most helpful type of feedback must be used by students.

In the following chapters, we will lay out our ideas about feedback and provide examples, metaphors, and approaches to thinking about critical issues.

AN EXAMPLE FROM THE CLASSROOM: HOW MUCH FEEDBACK AND ABOUT WHAT?

Donna Price and her colleagues (2017) conducted a study of her middle school English classes as part of her doctoral research. She asked students to prepare an essay and hand it in for marking. She provided individualized feedback to all students and then gave them the chance to revise their essays before receiving a grade. She found the students made substantial gains from their first essay to the revised version of it. So far so good. But what was surprising was what the students said about the process when she discussed it with them in focus groups. The first surprise Donna got was how enthusiastic students were about this process. She reported that the students told her that nobody had ever given them feedback and then let them work on their essays more before getting a grade. We heard similar sentiments in our own studies with university and high school students (Lipnevich et al., 2014; Lipnevich & Smith, 2009a, 2009b). Students are grateful to have a chance to use the feedback they receive and are eager to implement it to enhance their writing. So, no matter how spectacular the feedback you provide at the end of the course is, without giving students the opportunity and incentive to use this feedback, you may be sure that your effort was wasted. To reiterate, feedback can only be effective if students actively engage in it, understand it, and get the opportunity to try what they are doing again.

FEEDBACK ON FEEDBACK: ERROR AS INSIGHT

Here is a rather interesting mathematics problem that led to an obvious mistake. Martin has properly regrouped the number 583 into 400 + 170 + 13. Thus, he can perform the subtractions necessary to complete the problem. To our somewhat traditional approach to subtraction, it seems a bit cumbersome to do the problem this

(Continued)

(Continued)

way, but let's not worry about that. Martin has done everything correctly except for adding the numbers at the end instead of subtracting them.

What does this tell us, and how should we respond to Martin? We could just put an *X* on the problem and move on to the next problem. Or we could write a quick note to Martin saying that he added instead of subtracting. Or, we could ask Martin to see if he can find his mistake. Or, we could ask Martin to check all his work on this assignment and see if he wants to make any changes before getting a final grade. What would help Martin most?

As to what it tells us about Martin, we might conclude that it was just a brief lapse of concentration. But does it also tell us that Martin isn't careful about his work, or that he doesn't check to see if answers are reasonable, or that maybe Martin focuses too much on details and loses the main idea or goal? Do his answers on other problems confirm or disconfirm any of these hunches?

The second thing that came up in the discussions was equally important. They told her that they really appreciated how hard she worked on making comments, but it was really more than they could handle. They got a bit lost in all the feedback.

Two points here: The first is that students need to comprehend the feedback they receive and be able to translate their understanding into action. The second is that it is important to think seriously about how much feedback to give based on the learning goal of any given assignment or assessment. You cannot do everything at once. Humans have somewhat limited cognitive resources, and delivering too much information results in what scientists call a cognitive overload. If it's too extensive, students will be overwhelmed and overchallenged, and won't progress as much. With written work, we must always keep in mind the goal of the feedback. Too often we miss the message students are trying to communicate because of shortcomings in their communication skills. Teachers are often the only ones reading students' work, and we must be sure to comment on the ideas presented as well as the skill with which those ideas are communicated. Students' ideas deserve our respect and careful feedback along with clear opportunities for revision.

> *Students' ideas deserve our respect and careful feedback along with clear opportunities for revision.*

A FRAMEWORK FOR THINKING ABOUT FEEDBACK

As authors, we have given more workshops to teachers than we care to tally. We are academics by nature, and so we like to explain things, cite references and research studies, and consider the philosophical nature of things.

YES, BUT . . .

"Yes, but can you just show us how to do this?"

We will forsake our nature here and start this book out by providing you with a simple recipe for how to provide feedback. And here it is:

DISH: EFFECTIVE FEEDBACK

Ingredients:

- Care
- Planning
- Organization
- Follow-through
- Student focus
- Honesty
- Timeliness
- Clarity
- Insight
- Knowledge of the subject matter
- Pedagogical content knowledge (how to teach this content)
- Consideration of emotions that this message may elicit

Directions (see details in the text that follows):

- Plan your assessment.
- Give it to your students.
- Carefully consider what your students hand in.
- Craft a response.
- Provide students the opportunity and a reason to respond to your feedback.

We will discuss the "ingredients" in detail throughout this book. In some cases the meaning is clear: Honesty is honesty—we don't want to lie to our students. Some are not as straightforward. Take timeliness, for example. For burgeoning violinists, timeliness is critical. Teachers must deliver feedback on the spot, adjust the bow, and correct the string crossings. For more complex tasks, however, the timeliness of feedback is not important. In fact, delayed feedback is usually more effective on more complex tasks. Sometimes we need to take a break and do something else before returning, afresh, to the assignment we worked on. Interleaving, or alternating learning tasks, has been consistently shown to improve learning. So, please don't feel guilty if you are delaying your comments on students' essays until next week.

Please don't feel guilty if you are delaying your comments on students' essays until next week.

This, by the way, is the kind of research finding that makes us really happy. Now let's elaborate a bit on the directions:

Plan your assessment: Start by blending your knowledge of the subject matter with your pedagogical content knowledge and student focus, and generate a vehicle through which you can learn about your students' progress. This could be an assignment, a quiz, homework, or a performance. It should be something that will give your students an opportunity to show you what they can do and that will actively engage their abilities and enthusiasm. Also make sure it fits with your calendar. Will you be able to get it back to them in a timely fashion? Do you have them handing it in at the same time you are planning on a ninth birthday party for your son or daughter? Planning and organization are key here. And please note that you do not have to develop it yourself. There are lots of resources to go to in order to find a good assessment: colleagues, the internet, your files from past years. Teachers love to share. If you are having trouble or think your approach isn't all that you want, get help on this!

Give it to your students: Make sure you give students enough time to do a good job on the assessment, and to the degree possible, give them some choice in how they execute it. Make sure it fits with their calendar. What else do they have going on? And be certain to check your own calendar as well. When they hand this in, will you have the time to assess what they've done and provide good feedback? Make sure the directions are clear from the outset. One thing we have found that students truly dislike is if you change the requirements midstream. Student focus, planning, and care are key ingredients here.

Carefully consider what your students hand in: We recommend "reading while sitting on your hands" as a first pass on assignments. You can always work on grammar, spelling, arithmetic errors, and the like on a second pass. First, focus on what the basic idea of what the assessment was about. What have your students shown you with regard to what they know and can do? You should work toward understanding what generated the response they gave you. What strengths do you see that you can build on? Where there are weaknesses, what appears to be the origins of those difficulties? Insight, subject matter knowledge, and pedagogical content knowledge are important ingredients here.

Craft a response: Next, decide what you want to say to your students. Where is your focus? Be sure to include strengths. And then decide how you are going to say it. What would you want to receive if you were in their shoes? How would you put this to your own children (or nieces and nephews)? John Hattie recommends feedback that he calls "high-information," and we agree with this notion (Hattie & Timperley, 2007; Wisniewski et al., 2020). High-information feedback not only corrects mistakes; it gives the student strategies for avoiding them in the future, and sometimes ideas on when to use which strategies—more on that down the road a bit. Next, get the feedback presented in an organized fashion. This part of the recipe calls upon substantial measures of care,

The goal is almost always growth and an eye toward the future as opposed to making the current assignment as good as possible.

organization, and clarity, and do not forget honesty. It is possible to be kind and honest at the same time.

Provide students the opportunity and a reason to respond to your feedback: Complete the cycle! Let the students work on their skills. This might be on this assignment (maybe for an improved grade) or the next assignment. The goal is almost always growth and an eye toward the future as opposed to making the current assignment as good as possible.

SUMMARY AND TAKEAWAYS

In this chapter, we introduced our general view on feedback, provided some examples of good feedback, described issues that are encountered in providing feedback, and discussed a classroom example of feedback in action. Our focus is on student-centered feedback driven by concerns for student growth and well-being. For feedback to be effective, it has to be well designed by teachers, and well understood, engaged in, and acted on by students (see, e.g., Parr & Timperley, 2010). As teachers, we need to think carefully about what aspects of student learning and development we want to focus on in any given formative activity. How much feedback should we provide, on what should it focus, and what level of depth and detail is needed? How can we ensure that students "take on" the advice and feedback they are given? You do these things normally in your everyday teaching. But you can bring that perspective to providing feedback as well. You can think of instructional feedback simply in this way: *Instructional feedback is teaching based on current information.*

> Instructional feedback is teaching based on current information.

QUESTIONS TO CONSIDER

At the conclusion of each chapter, we provide a few questions for you to consider yourself and/or discuss with colleagues. Here are questions from this chapter:

1. How do you think about your students when you are providing feedback on their work?

2. What is your goal in providing feedback?

3. How stressful are time demands on you when marking papers and engaging in other forms of feedback?

4. When you provide feedback, is your focus on the work at hand, or do you think about future assignments/performance as well?

FEEDBACK FROM THE PERSPECTIVE OF THE LEARNER

In Chapter 1, we presented a "recipe" for providing feedback to students. Our purpose there was to give you an overall idea of what we are talking about in terms of teachers presenting feedback to students. In this chapter, we take a somewhat different approach. We look at feedback from the perspective of the learner—the recipient of the feedback. We've all been there. We were all students once, and we are all still learners today in many aspects of life. In this chapter, we will leave "the front of the class" and move to the students' seats to get a very different perspective on feedback. In doing so, we will look at a model of feedback that we proposed and recently revised that looks at the processes underlying feedback.

SETTING THE SCENE

Let's set the scene. Throughout this explanation of the model, we will shift back and forth between this scenario and an explanation of the model. We'll put the scenario in italics to make the transitions easier.

You are a seventh-grade student, and you have handed in a report on the Jamestown Colony that was settled in Virginia in the early 1600s. You were allowed to choose your topic for this assignment, and you were asked to provide a summary of your topic and what it might have been like to be a 12-year-old in that time and place. You were told that your grade would be based 40% on the accuracy and completeness of the details about your topic, 30% on how well you described being a young person in that setting, and 30% on writing style, grammar, punctuation, and spelling. You worked pretty hard on the report and believe you did a good job—maybe not great as you ran short of time at the end, but somewhere between good and very good. It's been a week since you handed the paper in, and the teacher is walking around the classroom, handing the reports back.

A MODEL OF RESPONSE TO INSTRUCTIONAL FEEDBACK

Figure 2.1 presents a model of how students receive and respond to instructional feedback. We'll use that as a basis for looking at feedback from the student's perspective.

The Context

Instruction happens in a context, and we define *context* very broadly. It may be culture, an academic domain, or an academic versus nonacademic setting—all of these would have an important influence over the entire student feedback process. For example, hearing

FIGURE 2.1   ■   A Student Feedback Interaction Model

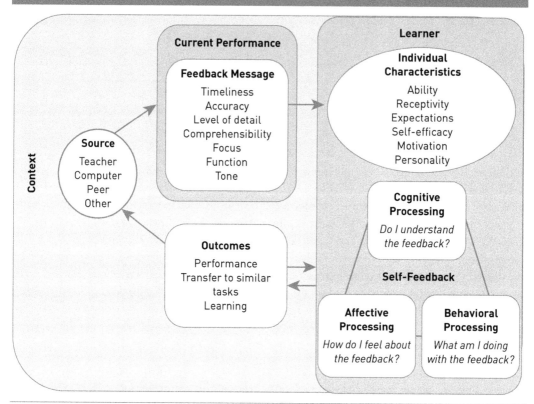

Source: Lipnevich and Smith (2022).

The "feedback culture" in the school also contextualizes the interactions of students with feedback.

"You can do so much better!" from your swimming coach will be perceived very differently compared to the exact same comment from your math teacher one day before you take a college entrance exam. The "feedback culture" in the school also contextualizes the interactions of students with feedback.

If students expect feedback, understand its purpose and value, and possess a set of tools that allow them to process it, the benefit (or the power!) of feedback will be so much greater.

The Source of the Feedback

The actual chain begins with the source of the feedback and the student's current performance. Let's start with the source, which in this case is your teacher. But the feedback could be coming from a computer, a peer, or perhaps the activity itself (if, for example, you are shooting an arrow or baking a cake). For most students, the teacher is a trusted source of instructional feedback, and usually a person with whom the student has a positive relationship. That relationship, and the trust that the student has in the teacher, is a key factor in the receipt and processing of feedback. Combined with beliefs in the nature and the quality of the task or assessment that is generating the feedback, the student's relationship with and trust in the teacher determines how the student will react to the feedback.

The student's relationship with and trust in the teacher determines how the student will react to the feedback.

Thus, the student has expectations, as well as an emotional anticipation. If the feedback received is consonant with the student's expectations, it will be welcomed. On the other hand, if the feedback is completely at odds with what the student is expecting, it can lead to a strong, negative emotional response, and perhaps a rejection of the feedback message.

Returning to our scenario, you have expectations and emotions concerning what you are about to receive. You might think that this will go well, and that you trust your teacher to "be on your side," and therefore you are eagerly awaiting the feedback. But maybe it is early in the school year, and this is the first assessment being handed back to you by this teacher. You like the teacher and believe he is fair, but you have no idea how he generates feedback.

This might cause some anxiety over what you are about to receive. Or perhaps you've already had a bad experience (in your view), and you have a substantial amount of anxiety as your teacher approaches your desk.

Source: istock.com/SeventyFour

Another potential source of feedback is peers. Peers can be involved in feedback, but as teachers, we are often reluctant to use this resource. Peer feedback has the potential of benefiting both the recipient and the provider.

Here, we should keep in mind that students need explicit guidelines on how to deliver feedback. We recommend offering students key words or phrases, such as "Can you tell me more about this?" or "I really like how you approached . . ." or "Let's think together about how to develop . . ." Similarly, clarifying goals and purposes of peer feedback activity will make it easier for students to accept comments from a peer. To go back to the context, this all is premised on a comfortable classroom atmosphere where learners are expected to help each other grow.

The Feedback Message

And now we move to the feedback message itself. What did the teacher say? How did the teacher say it? Was it presented in a timely fashion (for some tasks)? What was it about? Is it understandable? Did it say what to do next? It is truly remarkable how much feedback messages can vary from one teacher to another, from one assignment to another, and from one student to another. In our model, we list out timeliness, level of detail, comprehensibility, accuracy, tone, focus, and function as ways that feedback can vary. Let's explore those for a minute. With regard to timeliness, there are domains in which feedback should be presented as soon after the work is completed as possible. Take music or sports, for example. The feedback here has to be immediate in order to have its effect. It wouldn't make sense to say, "Evan, remember last week you didn't lift your right elbow enough when doing your taekwondo form?" The student needs to have this information immediately. On the other hand, when students are working on an essay or science project, receiving delayed feedback doesn't seem to affect outcomes much, studies show (Hattie & Timperley, 2007). Moreover, as we alluded to in Chapter 1, studies now show that interleaving is an excellent way to learn (Brown et al., 2014). So, especially with assignments that are longer and take more time for the students to work on, don't worry if you can't deliver students' papers at the next class meeting. Sometimes you will have to say, "Listen, folks, I will have these back to you after the Thanksgiving break." At the same time, don't overdo it either. You don't want your students to forget what the assignment was about.

Peer feedback has the potential of benefiting both the recipient and the provider.

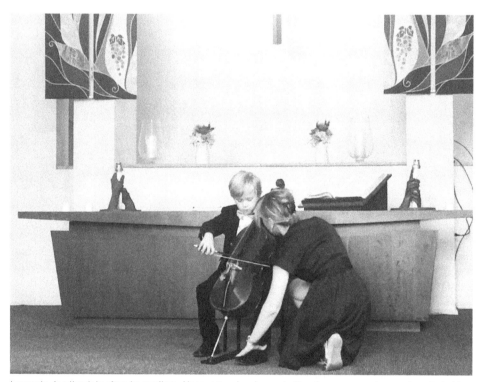

In music, feedback is often immediate. Here, a teacher is reminding the young performer how to hold the instrument.

Next we consider level of detail in the feedback. As we mentioned, we have to think about how detailed we are going to get with the feedback. In most cases, a good rule of thumb for this is that feedback should be proportional to the amount of effort the students put into the assignments.

That is not to say that you should write as much as the student did (!), but rather to point out that lengthier, more detailed assignments will call for more feedback from you than shorter ones.

Feedback should be proportional to the amount of effort the students put into the assignments.

The focus of the feedback is critical. It should be directly related to what you said the assignment was about—the rubric or the details provided in the description of the task. If this is a history assignment (as in our example), the feedback should primarily be about history and the goals of the lesson and not focus too much on spelling or grammar. One really important aspect of the feedback message is to not lose sight of the big picture and focus too much on details. Keep in mind that we are constantly on a quest to not overburden students' cognitive resources. If we do, our feedback will fail.

Feedback needs to be understood by the student, so it is important to consider how you are phrasing your comments and the level of vocabulary you use. Consider the students' level of expertise and prior knowledge and, if possible, vary your feedback by students. If you have a student with a lower level of language proficiency, maybe go lighter on bigger words and don't use as many. Feedback also needs to be accurate. This can be a real challenge at times, especially when you want to be encouraging but it is really hard to find a whole lot that went right in an assignment.

A HOT TAKE ON SCAFFOLDING

Scaffolding is a process of removing some of the complexity of a task so that the learner can focus more on the basics. In normal language, we call that "lending a hand." Often, when talking about scaffolding, we use an example of running alongside a person learning to ride a bike and holding the seat so that the bike doesn't fall over before the rider can get "up to speed" and get a sense of balance that comes with that higher speed. Then the "helper" gradually lets go of the bike seat (often without telling the rider). This removal of the support is "fading" and is based on feedback on the learner's progress. Scaffolding is usually attributed to Belarusian psychologist Lev Vygotsky (Puntambekar, 2022) although Maria Montessori (1949/2007) wrote about similar ideas prior to Vygotsky, as did Jerome Bruner (1961).

One of your authors encountered a great example of scaffolding a few years ago while taking a glassblowing class. As shown in the picture, you typically work on glass without gloves. The glass, at the end of a long rod, is somewhere around 1,800 degrees Fahrenheit. You have to roll the rod back and forth to keep the glass from falling off the rod in a lump. This is a version of rubbing your tummy and patting your head at the same time. The only difference is a pound of molten glass millimeters away from your unprotected fingers.

(Continued)

(Continued)

To help out as you are beginning to learn how to do this, the instructor takes charge of rolling the rod. He does it completely at first, then has you just place your left hand on the rod to get the feeling of it, then has you do so with more pressure, and finally removes his hand so you are doing it yourself. The picture shows the moment when he has released the rod.

What he has to do as a teacher is to track your progress on this technique and determine just how much support he needs to provide at all times. Feedback!

That glass is around 1,800 degrees Fahrenheit. No gloves!

This brings us to three really critical aspects of feedback: the focus, function, and tone of the feedback. Let's start with focus. What message is being sent to the student? What is the student being asked to concentrate on? Is the feedback essentially corrective in nature? Does it basically edit the student's work? Or does it suggest that there are errors to be found there and that the student should find them? The function relates to whether the feedback is primarily concerned with the current assignment, whether it is more forward-looking ("On your next essay, see if you can . . ."), or whether the sole purpose of the message is to motivate the student without focusing much on the content. The term *feedforward* has become popular in educational circles today, and although your authors are not particularly fond of neologisms, we've pretty much made our peace with this one. So the question here is whether you are more focused on the current work or where the student is headed in the future. Finally, there is the tone of the feedback. Is it fundamentally positive? Is it personal? Does it acknowledge past efforts and look forward to future ones? We deal with all these issues more extensively in Chapter 3, but it is worthwhile to consider them as we look at feedback from the student's perspective.

You receive your paper, and the first thing you notice is that there is no grade on it. Instead, it begins with a note written to you: "Maria, I found your report fascinating; I learned some things about Jamestown that I did not know, and I enjoyed reading about your ideas of what it would have been like to be a 12-year-old girl in Jamestown during the early 1600s. Here is where I'd like to see you go next on this assignment . . ." Your first reaction is maybe one of relief; Mr. Jackson liked your work. And the next emotion might be one of a bit of excitement: This is good, and it's not over. There is more work that you can do to make this better. Where might this be going? You take a quick flip through the remaining pages and see that Mr. Jackson has written you a number of smaller suggestions, and that there is little by way of editorial and grammatical corrections. You are feeling like you have a partner, an advisor, on your report. And you aren't really as focused on a grade as you were when Mr. Jackson was walking around the classroom, handing back the papers.

The Learners and Their Actions

Feedback is only effective if it is used. Feedback is only effective if it is used. (Yes, we said that twice. It's that important.) We now turn to the learner directly. Learners are different—from one another, from one subject area to the next, and from themselves at different points in time. They differ in their achievement levels with regard to the assessment at hand, in their overall receptivity to getting feedback, in their sense of self-efficacy and motivation, and in their expectations for the feedback they are about to receive. If you are teaching 22 children in an elementary school, you have a different set of circumstances than if you are teaching 112 in a high school. Elementary school teachers typically know their students on a more personal level than high school teachers (just due to sheer numbers and the amount of time interacting with them). This allows for more personalization of feedback messages and greater consideration of the factors just mentioned. But whatever the level of personalization, and no matter the number of students, what we want to see with regard to feedback is the student engaging with it.

We call these the ABCs of processing—affective, behavioral, cognitive—and encourage all feedback providers to consider them when crafting their feedback messages.

So now we turn to the learner directly. The feedback has been received, and it has to be processed by the learner: cognitively (making sense of it, understanding it), affectively (processing emotions elicited to the feedback received), and behaviorally (executing a plan of action based on the feedback). We call these the ABCs of processing—*affective, behavioral, cognitive*—and encourage all feedback providers to consider them when crafting their feedback messages.

How will the student feel, think, and behave in response to what you are saying? It may change the way you approach the feedback.

Let us imagine a situation where the feedback allows for continued work on the assessment, is informative about what to do next, and is respectful of each student's current efforts on the task. What then? Well, the learners (students) first need to understand what has been said. They need to be able to cognitively process the feedback. As they do that, they react to it from an emotional (affective) perspective. How do they feel about it? Does it match their expectations? If not, what do they do then? Do they reject the feedback or change their own assessment of their work? And after they have processed the information both cognitively and affectively, they must take a course of action with regard to working on it—that is, employ behavioral strategies.

The opportunity and motivation to revise are critical to students' use of feedback.

If it will not be handed in again, then there may be little motivation to work on it. On the other hand, if no grade has been assigned yet, and if it will be considered by the teacher again, then the motivation to work on it may be strong. In other words, the opportunity and motivation to revise are critical to students' use of feedback.

As you go through your work, you see: "Maria, I had a bit of difficulty on this part of the report. It is, well, a little bit 'clunky' if you know what I mean. It doesn't read smoothly like what precedes and follows this section. Maybe try focusing on what comes just before this and just after, and see if you can make it flow better." Now, do you agree with that or not? How do you feel about it? It clearly is what Mr. Jackson would like to see you work on, and you don't have a grade yet, so maybe it's a good idea to reread this section and see if you understand what he means and how you can improve it. Should you go talk to him about it or try to handle this all on your own? What else has he recommended you do on the report? How much time can you devote to this?

Outcomes

This is an aspect of the feedback process that is often overlooked. What do we get out of providing feedback? What do we want to get out of it? What does the student want to get out of it? It might be useful here to compare feedback in classrooms to feedback in sports coaching. On a report, if a student gets feedback, it can often just be viewed as "Well, this is what the teacher had to say about what I did." But on an athletic field (or in a music lesson), the feedback is specifically geared toward improvement. The learner knows that, and the coach knows that. There is a notion not of trying to improve the thing that is now over (the previous free throw attempt, the last singing of that passage of the song, etc.), but rather of how to make the next version better. For many things in sports, the event doesn't change. It's always about throwing the discus or making the free throw. But in the classroom, what is the equivalent of that? What do we (both the teacher and the student) want to see improve: the report itself, or the ability to do the report? This is sometimes referred to as the difference between *performance* (the current report, product, etc.) and *learning* (the knowledge and skills that can be taken on to the next activity), and it is an important difference, especially for considering how to provide feedback. Occasionally we are actually more interested in the current performance (maybe practicing a speech or working on a piece of art), but much more often we are looking to the future and are concerned about long-term learning.

It is a truism of schooling that students are often more interested in what grade they are going to receive than anything else, and we devote a whole chapter to grades as feedback later on, but we need to think about how the students view the additional work we would like them to do on this task. It has often been said that grades are the pay that teachers hand out for the work that they want students to do. This seems a bit harsh to us, but it is important to take the students' perspective in asking them to work on something, especially to take a second attempt at it. As educational researcher Jere Brophy once said, "Some kids will only work for grades, some because they like what they are doing and others to improve, but a lot of kids will just do the work because they buy into the notion of school. They aren't sure what they are getting in return, but they are willing to go along with the system" (Brophy, personal communication, 2007).

Having received the feedback from Mr. Jackson, you are now faced with the notion of what you want to get out of this assessment. How much more work should you put into it? What are your goals for this assessment at this point? Are the questions you are asking yourself more along the lines of "How can I make this as good as it can be?" or "How can I learn from this in order to make my next assessment better on the first draft?" or "How can I get the highest grade (perhaps combined with the least amount of work)?" Part of what you are thinking about might have to do with your relationship with Mr. Jackson. Do you want to show him what you can do, or is it good enough to just get by and be done with this assignment?

If, as a teacher, your primary concern with regard to outcomes is learning—improvement on the next task—then what can you do in terms of feedback to motivate the students toward that outcome? In part, we would argue that the key here is to take a long-term perspective on feedback and have it be an ongoing conversation with the students about their progress.

Take a long-term perspective on feedback and have it be an ongoing conversation with the students about their progress.

That would include noting progress as you see it and pointing to specific areas of growth you'd like to see in subsequent work. Furthermore, teachers may provide feedback on more general skills and dispositions and thus attempt to work on a broader notion of growth in their students. Time management, study strategies, teamwork—they all require feedback from the teacher in order to improve, and this feedback can be delivered along with the comments on the task or separately.

SUMMARY AND TAKEAWAYS

In this chapter, we looked at the complex interplay of student feedback components and turned the focus on feedback to the students' perspective: How do they understand the feedback messages they receive, how do they feel about them, and how do they choose to act on them? Taking that perspective has highlighted the fact that the nature of the message is critical with respect to how it is received and acted upon. Also critical is the nature of the relationship between the student and the teacher. Does the student believe that the teacher is "on their side" in this journey? The belief that the teacher is more an advocate than a judge is critical to a strong teaching and feedback-providing relationship.

QUESTIONS TO CONSIDER

1. How can you "take the student perspective" in providing feedback?

2. How can you ensure that your students will read your feedback, work on that feedback, and apply it on their next assessment?

3. How can you be certain that your students always understand what you are trying to say in your feedback?

4. How beneficial might it be to think about what you are going to say to students in their feedback *before* you develop the assessment or assignment that is going to generate that feedback?

5. Have you considered the ABCs of processing?

3 CHARACTERISTICS OF EFFECTIVE FEEDBACK MESSAGES

As teachers, when we sit down to mark a set of papers from our students, we often "dive right into" the task at hand. After all, we've done this a thousand times before. But it might be worthwhile, every now and then, to take a step back and think about the messages we are about to send to our students. How are those messages going to be received? How will they make our students feel? What are we asking them to do with this feedback (if anything)? Remember the ABCs from Chapter 2? Might there be a different or better way to do this? Are we actually in the right frame of mind? In this chapter, we will take that step back and look at the characteristics of feedback—look at the options that are open to us, and see if, maybe, we want to take a different approach.

GOALS

We might begin by thinking about our goals related to the feedback message to be delivered. What do we want to accomplish in our communications to the students? This is a very important aspect of providing feedback and perhaps one that we tend to overlook when contemplating a large stack of papers that need to be marked. It can be very worthwhile to ask yourself a few questions before beginning:

1. What did I ask the students to do here? (How did they perceive this assignment?)

2. What opportunity does this assignment provide for students to show me what they know and can do? (Might some students have been limited in what they could show—perhaps because they were not familiar with the subject matter of the assignment—but really have the underlying skills?)

3. What kind of feedback will produce the most growth in the students? (Should I focus on their strengths here or on areas that need improvement?)

4. What do I want students to do with this feedback? (How can I be clear in communicating to students what their next steps should be? Should I have them revise and hand in this assignment again?)

5. Are there areas that I shouldn't worry about in marking this assignment? (How can I make sure I don't overwhelm the students?)

Starting the process of providing feedback with a clear sense of what you want to accomplish can make you not only more effective in your feedback, but more efficient as well as you will be clearly focused on your goals.

CONTEXT

Feedback is typically provided following some kind of assignment, assessment, or performance on the part of the student. It could be a science lab, a one-on-one reading assessment, or a midterm examination in a foreign language course. How much of the emphasis of this assignment/assessment/performance is summative (related to grading in this case), and how much is formative (focused on student improvement)? We look at the issues of grading versus commentary extensively in Chapter 6.

PRACTICALITY

One of the authors of this book was once giving a professional development workshop to a gathering of high school English teachers. After listening to this author's detailed presentation on the many ways that one can look at and respond to an essay with rich and full descriptions of potential feedback, a teacher at the back of the room raised his hand and said . . .

YES, BUT . . .

"Yes, but you do realize I have 125 students."

The practicality question with regard to feedback is "How do I provide the best possible feedback to students given my time and resource constraints?"

And that is a critical issue with regard to providing feedback. In his mastery learning theory, Bloom (1971) emphasized that an ideal instructional setting was one student working with a skilled teacher. But that is simply not the situation that any teacher realistically faces (Bloom recognized this problem and developed approaches to get as close to it as possible). So the practicality question with regard to feedback is "How do I provide the best possible feedback to students *given my time and resource constraints?*"

In other words, "How do I stay sane?" In Chapter 7, we provide a number of approaches that are very helpful to students and very economical in terms of teacher time and resources. But for now, we will simply remain mindful of how much time a teacher can dedicate to providing feedback.

FEEDBACK AS CONVERSATION

Feedback should be thought of, and structured, as an ongoing conversation between the student and the teacher (Lipnevich & Smith, 2018; Winstone & Carless, 2019).

There is a tendency to think of feedback as a kind of "one-off" activity that is tied to an assignment or assessment that students hand in. And in many instances, that is true. In some, in fact, it is *necessary* (such as in large lecture classes at the university level). But it doesn't have to be in every case. Instead, feedback should be thought of, and structured, as an ongoing conversation between the student and the teacher (Lipnevich & Smith, 2018; Winstone & Carless, 2019).

The nature of the conversation typically begins with the teacher setting a task/assignment/assessment and the student responding to it. Then the teacher provides feedback on what has been handed in, and the student can revise and resubmit it as the conversation continues. Now, the idea of conversation is not always actionable with feedback, but it does provide a useful metaphor to consider in thinking about learning as an ongoing process, and one that involves both teacher and learner engaged in the same journey.

Before looking at all the options available to us for feedback, let's look at a simple example of providing feedback from an answer to a question from a biology test.

AN EXAMPLE FROM BIOLOGY

Consider an answer to the question from a ninth-grade biology test on viruses and bacteria as presented in Figure 3.1. Miranda has drawn representations of a virus and a bacterium. So, what is important here? What is being assessed? What kinds of suggestions/comments/advice will be the most productive for Miranda? Will certain approaches build her confidence and increase her interest in biology as a field of study? On this question, the teacher wants to know if students understand the differences in the structure of viruses and bacteria and, secondarily, if they know how to make drawings of the objects they learn about in biology.

FIGURE 3.1 ■ Miranda's Response to the Biology Assignment

Viruses and bacteria have many important differences. Draw a picture of each and label the important parts in your drawing. Separate the two drawings by boxing them out.

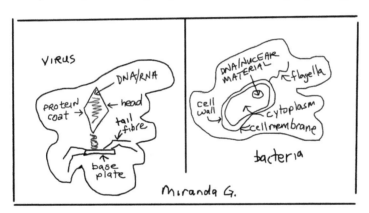

Now let's look at some possible comments a teacher might make to Miranda. In this case, the teacher is focused on the fact that Miranda has encircled her drawings with a line.

1. *Don't draw a line around everything. It's confusing.*

2. *What's the line for?*

3. *Miranda, the lines you have encircling everything kind of makes it look like they are parts of the cell. Probably best to leave them off in the future.*

4. *I understand that the line you have around everything is to kind of close it all in. But a tough marker on the state testing program might think that you think those labels belong in the cell. Think "like your marker" when laying out your answers on the test. Make it simple for them!*

Comment 1 is corrective in nature, simple and straightforward, present oriented, impersonal, and neutral to negative in tone. It is pretty easy to understand, but sends a message of "I'm in charge here and this is wrong." If there is a strong relationship between the student and the teacher, this might be OK as a comment, but it is a bit harsh. Comment 2 is very simple, indirect, oriented toward the process the student used, fairly impersonal, and indirectly action oriented. It is there to make the student think about the line. But it might be unclear as there are a lot of lines on the diagram. Which one is the teacher referring to? Comment 3 is at the level of the task (doesn't suggest any general strategy, just says not to draw a line around things here), easy to understand, personal (uses the student's name), future oriented, and action oriented. It is delivered with a soft tone ("probably best") and is dialogic in nature (suggests an ongoing conversation with the student). Comment 4 is made at what would be called a "metacognitive" level; that is, it takes an overarching look at Miranda's approach that can be applied in many settings, rather than just the particulars of this problem (for more on that, see the discussion of level in the Cognitive section of this chapter). It is personal in tone (uses *I* and *you*), forward looking, and dialogical in nature. It takes what can be seen as a correction and turns it into "Here's a hint between you and me."

CHARACTERISTICS OF FEEDBACK MESSAGES: A TAXONOMY

Now we look at the possibilities for feedback in a more systematic fashion. There is a lot of material in the following sections, and it might seem a bit overwhelming at first. But don't read it as a set of instructions or "must-haves." Instead, look at it as a set of possibilities. Do you want to personalize feedback by putting the student's name on a comment ("See if you can find an error or two in this section, Roberto")? Do you want to refer back to a previous assignment or anticipate a future one ("Real improvement here, Mark! Keep it up on your next essay")? Do you want to provide a corrective statement to the student, and also suggest how to avoid the error in the future ("You've got a simple arithmetic error here; see if you can correct it, and think about whether your current answer seems reasonable given the problem")? So think of the list of characteristics presented and explained as follows as options or possibilities for making your feedback stronger and more effective.

To begin, we ask the question, "How complex can feedback be?" Are you writing a quick comment, taking the time to provide a slightly longer one, or just marking something as right or wrong? Well, if you think about it (and your authors spend *way* too much time thinking about such things), it can be any of these, but also something much more complex.

In our work (Murray et al., 2018), we have looked at how feedback messages might differ and have come up with quite a few ways that they do. We have turned them into a bit of a taxonomy here. There are three broad levels—cognitive, affective, and behavioral—and then a number of subcategories under each. They parallel the behaviors of the student receiving feedback in Chapter 2 (once again, the ABCs). These various categories are not intended as some sort of prescription; they are just provided so that you can see how many different options you have in feedback messages, and to offer some thoughts about what might be most efficacious in any given setting.

MARKING, GRADING, AND SCALES

In most U.S. contexts, the terms *marking* and *grading* are used interchangeably. Sometimes we think of marking as a kind of quaint way of saying grading. But in other locations around the world, the two terms refer to different activities. *Marking* is what is done to come up with a numerical score for an assessment and to put comments (feedback!) on the papers. *Grading* refers to putting a letter grade on the assessment. Also, in many countries, what counts as an A, B, C, and so on is not up to the discretion of the teacher, but is determined by a fixed scale. A very common one is the following:

$$90-100 = \text{A+}$$
$$85-89 = \text{A}$$
$$80-84 = \text{A}-$$
$$75-79 = \text{B+}$$
$$70-74 = \text{B}$$
$$65-69 = \text{B}-$$
$$60-64 = \text{C+}$$
$$55-59 = \text{C}$$
$$50-54 = \text{C}-$$
$$\text{Below } 50 = \text{F}$$

Now, you might be thinking, "Fifty is a pass? How can that be? On a four-option multiple-choice test, 25% would be random guessing!" Most of the countries that employ such scales use very few multiple-choice items and are strict markers on essay tests.

COGNITIVE

The first broad category is cognitive. Feedback messages differ in the type of cognitive response that they engender and vary according to level, complexity, and student expertise. Here are the subcategories under cognitive:

Level

The first subcategory is level. Taken from the pioneering work on feedback of John Hattie and Helen Timperley (2007), this is probably the single most important way of looking at

Feedback messages differ in the type of cognitive response that they engender and vary according to level, complexity, and student expertise.

feedback. Hattie and Timperley provide four different levels of feedback: task, process, metacognitive (or self-regulatory), and personal. We describe these as follows.

- *Task:* Feedback at the task level is essentially just marking things as right or wrong. An *X* on a wrong answer on a math problem and the correction of a subject–verb agreement are examples of feedback at the task level.

- *Process:* Feedback at the process level points the student to the process that was used that the teacher wants to comment on. This might be on the order of "See if you can find the error you've made in this sentence" or "Please check your arithmetic on this problem." It doesn't provide the correct answer, but suggests that the student can do so.

- *Metacognitive:* Metacognition is literally "thinking about one's thinking." Metacognitive processes involve sitting back and reflecting on what we've done. Hattie and Timperley argue that this level of feedback (along with process-oriented feedback) is often the most beneficial. An example of metacognitive feedback might be "It's always good to put an assignment 'down' for a day or two and then come back and reread your work. Try to take the perspective of your audience when you do so."

- *Personal:* Hattie and Timperley's final level is called the personal level. They made it last not because they thought it was the best, but rather because they thought it was the broadest. It doesn't have to do with metacognitive behavior; instead, it speaks to the person as a whole. This often involves the notion of praise, such as "You're a really good writer. Congratulations on this!" Research on praise has almost always shown that it has a negative effect on student work. This seems counterintuitive, but we see it time and again. For a good review of the use of praise in teaching in general, see Brophy (1981; this reference is a bit dated, but it is really excellent). Praise tends to focus on the student and not the work, and it often suggests that success results not from the work the student puts in on an assessment, but rather from a natural ability that doesn't require work.

In looking at these four levels, one might be tempted to think that feedback can be given at one level and not the others, but that is not the case. Feedback can be given at multiple levels; in fact, Hattie and Timperley (2007) and Wisniewski et al. (2020) argue that the most effective feedback is what they call "high-information feedback." High-information feedback contains information on the task (right/wrong, weak/strong, could be improved), but also on the strategies used on the task and the self-regulation used in determining and applying strategies. And, this only makes sense. This is feedback that shows the learners what they did wrong, how to avoid the mistake in the future, and how to look to see when they should use that more effective strategy.

Hattie and Timperley (2007) and Wisniewski et al. (2020) argue that the most effective feedback is what they call "high-information feedback."

"STEPPING UP" YOUR FEEDBACK: HIGH-INFORMATION FEEDBACK

According to Hattie and Timperley (2007) and Wisniewski et al. (2020), the strongest feedback is "high-information feedback." This approach to feedback tells the student not only where an error was made (or, more broadly, where something could be improved), but also how to go about doing better the next time, as well as how to see where "the next time is" and what strategy to apply.

Let's look at this in action. We'll pick a somewhat unusual task, one of making art. Students were given a model of a kiwi bird and asked to make a pencil drawing of it. Here is the model given and one student's efforts.

Source: istock.com/GlobalP

Now, there is a tendency to look at any art made by a child and simply want to enjoy what they have done and congratulate them on their work. But that makes the assumption that what you are seeing is just what they wanted to produce and that they aren't interested in improving their skills. So let's put aside the natural tendency toward "Isn't that lovely?" and think about how we might help students improve their drawing skills.

In this instance, if possible, it would probably be better to talk to the student about the drawing because reference can be made to the model, and the teacher can check for understanding. "High-information" feedback might go as follows:

"I like your drawing, Ben. You've filled up the page with it, and you've got the proportions of the head and the body just about perfect. Now let's look at some places you might work on. You've got those dark eyes nice, but unless you were looking straight on at the front of the kiwi, you wouldn't see both of them at the same time. Let's look at this model. See how you only see one of the eyes when looking at it from this angle? Also, you've got the kiwi's long nose coming out of the side of its head. Let me show you a trick here. You can have it coming right out of the front by simply starting your drawing of the nose from within the head rather than on the side. Give it a try. Don't worry about going over lines. You can always erase those with a pencil drawing. One way you can really work on your

(Continued)

(Continued)

drawing is to spend more time looking at what you want to draw. Draw what you are actually seeing rather than what you think something should look like. Keep up your work!"

This feedback starts by pointing out some of the things Ben has done well, and then provides two specific correctives (eyes and nose). The teacher then shows Ben how to correct those, and gives him a strategy for working on those mistakes. She also gives him a broad strategy for art in general ("spend more time looking").

This is high-information feedback.

Corrective

The next subcategory under cognitive is corrective. To a degree, this might be considered part of the task aspect of the level subcategory, but it is so prevalent in feedback that it deserves its own subcategory. Corrective feedback occurs when we make a correction on the student's paper, marking something as wrong or less than desirable. Oftentimes, this simply involves editing the student's work or providing the right answer. It might go as far as showing the student how to do the problem (or write the sentence, or do the titration) properly. Corrective feedback is particularly good for students who are learning something new and need to know what they have right and wrong.

Corrective feedback is particularly good for students who are learning something new and need to know what they have right and wrong.

It's great if it can be combined with higher-level feedback.

Complexity

Complexity relates to two aspects of feedback messages. The first is how complex the feedback is, and the second is how complex the message is. The underlying issue is the same in both cases: Will the student understand the message? Sometimes the feedback we send can simply be too complex for the student to understand.

Sometimes the feedback we send can simply be too complex for the student to understand.

We might be trying to explain the use of the semicolon as a conjunction when the student doesn't really understand independent clauses. The feedback is simply beyond the student's grasp. At other times, we may be using vocabulary that the student doesn't understand. If we say, for example, that the addends don't total properly, the student might not know that we are referring to the numbers that need to be added up. The issue here is very straightforward: Does the student understand what we are saying?

Direction

Directionality in feedback is critical, and really needs to be thought through. In our feedback, are we trying to help the student work on the task at hand, or trying to encourage learning that will stay with the student and be usable in the future? Is the feedback really feed*back*, or do we really want feed*forward*, looking at future performance? Sometimes we are, in fact, working on the task at hand. Playing a piece of music for a recital, sanding down a wooden box in a woodshop, decorating a cake for an event, and working on a written piece for a publication are all examples of working on the task at hand. But often what we really want is for the student to "get it right the next time." In that case, we should try to craft a feedback message that focuses the student's attention on the next instance of what is under consideration—for example, "What is a good way to figure out when to use *me* and when to use *myself*?" (as opposed to simply correcting a mistake on the current paper).

We should try to craft a feedback message that focuses the student's attention on the next instance of what is under consideration.

AFFECTIVE

The second broad category is the affective aspect of the feedback. How does the feedback make the student feel? What is the emotion associated with the student's response to the feedback?

Tone

The first subcategory here is tone. The tone of the feedback can range from negative to neutral to positive. It's the same notion of tone as might exist in any communication. The concern is that so often our feedback is corrective in nature. Pointing out mistakes has a natural tendency to be negative in tone, so it is critical to try to be more positive, or at least neutral, when we do so.

Pointing out mistakes has a natural tendency to be negative in tone, so it is critical to try to be more positive, or at least neutral, when we do so.

Consider the differences in the following three feedback messages:

1. "The subject and verb don't agree here. Try dropping out the phrase that separates them and see how it sounds. This can be tricky!"

2. "Watch your subject–verb agreement. If you read it without the phrase in between them, you might see the problem."

3. "Subject–verb agreement error. Take out the middle phrase and you'll see your mistake."

These differences might seem subtle, but note that the first comment speaks directly to the student and it is clear that the message is coming from the teacher. Also, the comment says that the solution can be tricky, which communicates that this is a problem for lots of people, maybe the teacher included, and not just the student. The second message is fairly neutral. It does put the error on the student, but it expresses confidence in the student's ability to find it. The third message begins with a corrective; it basically says, "You made a mistake here." It emphasizes the student error with the final phrase *your mistake*.

Interpersonal

Feedback that is interpersonal communicates the teacher's acknowledgment of a relationship with the student—that they are in "this learning thing" together. A common way to accomplish this is to use the student's name. It can be as simple as the difference between "You can do this" and "You can do this, Bill." It might also make reference to a shared experience or previous comment (from a different assessment) that acknowledges that the teacher is thinking about the learner as a person. For example, "Your diagram here is a real improvement from the one in your last assignment." In addition to commenting on the quality of the diagram, it lets the student know that you remember their work and are glad to see their improvement. You care.

Feedback that is interpersonal communicates the teacher's acknowledgment of a relationship with the student—that they are in "this learning thing" together.

Praise

Praise is a conundrum. The research literature shows fairly consistently that praise doesn't seem to be helpful to students, and in fact is often associated with doing less well if they get it than if they don't. How can that be? Who doesn't like to hear, "Good job!"? And yet, the research is pretty clear that it is typically not helpful (see, e.g., Hattie & Timperley, 2007; Lipnevich & Smith, 2009a), particularly when the feedback simply tells the student how good they are in a given subject area: "You're such a good writer, Susan!" Brummelman (2020) edited a whole book on praise, and the conclusion appears to be "It's complicated!" Some students dislike being praised, whereas others crave it. Effort-level praise seems to positively contribute to performance, whereas ability praise may prevent students from taking risks. Praise may "anchor" students on the positive message, and they may feel less motivated to engage in any kind of revisions. After all, "I am terrific already—why bother?" However, it seems to be safe to deliver praise at the end of the unit or make it very specific and about work, not the student.

Deliver praise at the end of the unit or make it very specific and about work, not the student.

BEHAVIORAL

With regard to feedback at the behavioral level, we do *not* mean trying to improve student misbehavior. There is feedback there as well, but for us, that is much more an issue of classroom management. Behavior feedback is interactive in nature, or directs the students to particular behaviors in which to engage.

Dialogical

Dialogical feedback is simply feedback that engages the student in a conversation or dialog. It is feedback that may refer to a previous assessment/assignment, or that refers to something the teacher and student have talked about before. It anticipates a response from the student and supposes that there is a back-and-forth conversation going on. Examples of this might include the following:

Behavior feedback is interactive in nature, or directs the students to particular behaviors in which to engage.

1. "I'm not sure what you were going for here. Maybe you could . . ."
2. "Do you remember when we discussed asking yourself if the answer could possibly look like this? Is this at all reasonable?"
3. "Yes! This is exactly what I meant when I said that . . ."

Action-Oriented

Action-oriented feedback directs the student to next steps to be taken. It addresses the critical feedback question of "Where do we go from here?" It's the sort of feedback that begins with "Here's what I would like you to do next on this." When the teacher and student have a strong relationship, feedback of this type doesn't have to have a reward attached to it other than "Let's see if we can make this better." If, however, you have over 100 students in your classes and maybe it's the beginning of the year, you aren't going to have such relationships. That is where you might employ an approach of having an assignment handed in, feedback (of some sort) provided, and the second draft, not the first draft, count for the grade. That provides a strong motivation (external, but still strong) to take the feedback and really engage in it. (See more on this idea in Chapter 7.)

SUMMARY AND TAKEAWAYS

There has been a lot to absorb in this chapter, and we agree it might be a bit overwhelming. In terms of thinking about the nature of your feedback messages, perhaps these are the key issues to consider:

1. Is the feedback you are giving "high-information"?
2. Does it provide strategies and ways of thinking about the task at hand that will help the student in the future?
3. Does it communicate to the student that "you are on their side" in this learning thing?
4. Does it give the student an opportunity and the motivation to work on the feedback you've provided?
5. Is your feedback something you would appreciate receiving if you were the learner?

QUESTIONS TO CONSIDER

1. How can you develop a system for reviewing and thinking about the feedback messages you send?

2. If you asked your students about what kind of feedback they would like to get, what do you think they would say? Why not ask them?

3. Look at a feedback comment you've made, and then add the student's name to it. How does that change the feel of the message?

4. How often are your feedback messages forward looking?

5. How often do you write feedback messages that, in Hattie's terminology, are "high-information"?

4 WHAT IS FEEDBACK?

In this chapter, we take a step back to look at the history of feedback and describe why it's such an important part of classroom teaching. The significance of feedback in learning has actually been recognized for centuries. Its roots can be found in the writings of early education theorists such as John Amos Comenius, Johann Heinrich Pestalozzi, and Johann Friedrich Herbart (Bloom, 1974). Although these famous scholars defined feedback in slightly different ways, all recognized its essential value in the teaching and learning process. A well-written account of the history of feedback and how it relates to educational issues today is Dylan Wiliam's 2018 essay on the topic. It's well worth reading, and we encourage you to take a look at it.

Our focus in this chapter is to briefly review that history, paying special attention to how the definition of feedback has evolved in recent years. We then consider the vital role modern versions of feedback play in the instructional process, and how it contributes to student success.

A BRIEF HISTORY OF FEEDBACK

Most modern education theorists can trace their ideas on feedback to the pioneering work of Benjamin S. Bloom. In his seminal 1968 article, "Learning for Mastery," Bloom described how teachers' classroom assessments could be used as learning tools, rather than just as evaluation devices for grading students and certifying their competence. To emphasize this different purpose, Bloom recommended they be called *formative* assessments, borrowing a term that Michael Scriven (1967) coined to describe "in-progress" program evaluations that focused on improving programs during the implementation process rather than simply verifying how good or poor they were at the end.

For students, the feedback showed what they had mastered to that point and what ideas, skills, or processes required more work.

Bloom (1968) defined formative assessments as "diagnostic-progress" instruments designed to provide both students and teachers with information on what concepts and skills have been learned well and which need additional time and study. He referred to this diagnostic information as "feedback" (p. 6). For students, the feedback showed what they had mastered to that point and what ideas, skills, or processes required more work. For teachers, it clarified what instructional activities had worked well and what parts of their teaching needed revision or modification. Bloom was quick to add, however, that diagnostic feedback alone was unlikely to result in improved learning *unless* it was accompanied by "prescriptive" information about what students should do to remedy their learning difficulties.

In other words, simply going over assessments with students, identifying which responses were correct and incorrect or which criteria were met and not met, seldom yields much improvement. To better their performance, Bloom stressed that students need guidance and direction from teachers on *how* to improve. He referred to this prescriptive guidance as "corrective" activities.

Feedback alone was unlikely to result in improved learning unless it was accompanied by "prescriptive" information about what students should do to remedy their learning difficulties.

Bloom further emphasized that corrective activities should *not* be simply reteaching, a process that typically involves repeating the same instructional activities a second time and hoping for better results. Instead, corrective activities must offer students alternative ways to learn. Specifically, they must present the concepts and skills differently and engage students in different ways than did the original instruction. Bloom recommended that teachers link the corrective activities to specific items or prompts on the formative assessments so students need to study only the particular concepts and skills with which they're having difficulty. In this way, correctives are individualized, based on each student's unique learning needs. As we noted in Chapter 3, Hattie and Timperley (2007) described the same idea as "high-information feedback."

Correctives are individualized, based on each student's unique learning needs.

Bloom believed that the combination of "feedback with correctives," provided through regular formative assessments paired with specific guidance for correcting learning errors, would help nearly *all* students experience learning success. Altogether, this provided the basis for the instructional process Bloom (1971) called "mastery learning." It also became the foundation for instructional improvement programs worldwide.

Numerous researchers and program developers took up Bloom's ideas when designing new approaches to teaching and learning. One prominent example is *Understanding by Design* (UbD) created by Grant Wiggins and Jay McTighe (2004). In developing UbD, however, Wiggins and McTighe had concerns about the word *correctives* because it could be interpreted as teachers or coaches instructing students on the "correct" way of improving their performance. Although this connotation worked for some learning goals (e.g., correctly using a formula in math or using the right grammar in an essay), they believed it was less appropriate for other goals. For example, is there a "correct" way for students to make revisions to their creative story or to support a persuasive argument? Is there a "correct" way for a group of students to prepare their final project presentation? Wiggins and McTighe (2007) suggested that terms such as *guidance, suggestions, recommendations*, and *advice* would be more broadly applicable than *correctives*, and settled on *feedback with guidance* in describing this aspect of UbD.

The combination of "feedback with correctives," provided through regular formative assessments paired with specific guidance for correcting learning errors, would help nearly all students experience learning success.

COMBINING DIAGNOSIS AND PRESCRIPTION

In their article "The Power of Feedback," John Hattie and Helen Timperley (2007) initially describe feedback in the same way Bloom (1968) did nearly 40 years earlier, focusing on its essential "diagnostic" nature. They define feedback as "information provided by an agent (teacher, peer, book, parent, self, experience) regarding aspects of one's performance or understanding" (Hattie & Timperley, 2007, p. 81). They also address the need to pair this "diagnostic" information with "prescriptive" corrective activities, stating, "A teacher or parent can provide *corrective information*, a peer can provide an alternative strategy, a book can provide information to clarify ideas, a parent can provide encouragement, and a learner can look up the answer to evaluate the correctness of a response or understanding" (Hattie & Timperley, 2007, p. 81).

But later in their discussion, Hattie and Timperley (2007) alter their definition of feedback to include *both* diagnostic and prescriptive features:

> However, when feedback is combined with more a correctional review, the feedback and instruction become intertwined until "the process itself takes on the forms of new instruction, rather than informing the student solely about correctness" (Kulhavy, 1977, p. 212). To take on this instructional purpose, feedback needs to provide information specifically relating to the task or process of learning that fills a gap between what is understood and what is aimed to be understood (Sadler, 1989). (p. 82)

Hattie and Timperley go on to describe feedback as the "second part" of teaching. The first part involves teachers' initial instruction to impart new knowledge and skills, combined with assessment procedures to evaluate students' understanding and level of mastery. The second part—the feedback—relates to three major questions:

1. Where am I going?

2. How am I going?

3. Where to next?

According to Hattie and Timperley (2007), these three questions address the dimensions of "feed up," "feed back," and "feed forward" (p. 88).

"Where am I going?" relates to the learning goals or destination. It tells students what they're expected to learn and be able to do after engaging in a particular set of learning tasks. "How am I going?" describes what progress students have made toward those goals. In other words, it tells students exactly where they are on their learning journey. "Where to next?" identifies what activities students should undertake to make better progress. It clarifies what students need to do in order to achieve the learning goals and reach their destination.

A study by John Hattie and a team of colleagues (2021) asked more than 3,000 high school and college students which of these

While diagnostic information about what was done well and what areas need additional work is helpful, improvement requires useful, specific, and actionable guidance provided by the teacher.

three feedback components they found most helpful in improving essays they submitted online. Not surprisingly, students consistently preferred the prescriptive "Where to next?" information. Just as Bloom (1968) suggested when he first described this process, while diagnostic information about what was done well and what areas need additional work is helpful, improvement requires useful, specific, and actionable guidance provided by the teacher.

What's next for me?

Source: istock.com/katleho Seisa

A CHANGE IN DEFINING QUESTIONS

To describe the three dimensions of feedback in this book, we return to the descriptive phrases initially used by Benjamin Bloom (1968, 1971) and his mentor, Ralph W. Tyler (1949). To us, these descriptions are clearer and more in line with the language of today's teachers. In particular, we've chosen to describe each dimension with a "What?" question rather than "Where?" or "How?"

Instead of "Where am I going?" we use "What are the learning goals?" This identifies students' destination in their learning journey. In most cases, learning goals are described in a school's curriculum that outlines what all students should learn and be able to do at the completion of each elementary grade level or particular secondary courses. Although educators and subject-area experts are typically the ones who specify the learning goals in the curriculum, students are sometimes given opportunities to select their own, individualized learning goals.

Instead of "How am I going?" we use "What have I learned?" This is the diagnostic aspect of feedback that describes what each student has mastered in terms of the learning goals, and what areas need additional study and work. It identifies for students how far they have progressed in their journey toward achieving the learning goals and where they are on their learning continuum.

Finally, instead of "Where to next?" we use "What's next?" This describes the third and most crucial aspect of feedback. It is that vital component that shifts attention from diagnosis to prescription. "What's next?" provides students with specific guidance and direction on the steps they need to take to remedy any learning difficulties, correct any errors, and master any remaining elements in order to achieve the learning goals.

In our descriptions of feedback, you will find that we also stress Bloom's idea that "What's next?" cannot be simply reteaching or repetition of the same learning activities. We cannot simply require students to "Do it again, and this time we'll hope for better results!" Instead, the guidance and direction we offer our students must present the concepts and ideas differently and engage students in ways that are qualitatively different from what we did in our initial teaching.

Feedback is teaching based on knowledge of student progress.
Source: istock.com/ibnjaafar

Therefore, the three major questions that we believe need to be addressed in feedback and that we will continue to emphasize throughout this book are these:

1. What are the learning goals?

2. What have I learned?

3. What's next?

Similar to the questions set out by Hattie and Timperley (2007), our first two questions deal with the diagnostic aspects of feedback while the third addresses that important prescriptive element. The meaning we attach to these three defining questions of feedback is the same as nearly all researchers emphasize (see Lipnevich & Smith, 2018). These aspects of feedback contribute most to its effectiveness in all teaching and learning contexts. Our rewording is intended simply to clarify meaning and align our discussions with the language most teachers use today. We hope these changes serve those purposes well.

SUMMARY AND TAKEAWAYS

The premises of instructional feedback can be traced to the pioneering work of Benjamin S. Bloom (1968) who brought the term *formative assessment* to education and described how the use of regular checks on students' learning progress could be used to identify students' learning difficulties. Bloom further stressed that to improve students' learning, the diagnostic "feedback" provided to students by formative assessments must be paired with prescriptive "corrective" activities designed to help students remedy their learning difficulties. Decades later, modern writers, including Hattie and Timperley (2007), combined these diagnostic and prescriptive elements to form three major questions to be addressed by instructional feedback. In the language of today's teachers, these three questions are as follows:

1. What are the learning goals?

2. What have I learned?

3. What's next?

The answer to the first question describes the specific learning goals that make up students' learning destination; that is, what are students expected to learn and be able to do? The answer to the second question identifies what students have currently achieved and where additional work is needed. In other words, it describes where students are presently in their learning journey. The answer to the third question provides students with guidance and direction in remedying their learning difficulties to achieve their learning goals and reach their learning destination.

By providing answers to these three questions in the feedback we offer to students, we can better guide *all* our students to learning success. As a result of that success, students will feel better about themselves as learners, more confident in learning situations, and better equipped to handle future learning challenges.

QUESTIONS TO CONSIDER

1. Were you surprised to learn the vital importance of instructional feedback was identified by Benjamin Bloom over a half century ago? Why do you think it hasn't become more common practice in education today?

2. Have you ever experienced assessments as true learning tools that helped you learn better? Did your teachers ever follow assessments with instructional activities designed to help you improve any learning errors you made?

3. How do you think your students will respond to the idea of using assessment results to actually help them learn better and become successful learners?

4. Among the three questions to be addressed in instructional feedback, which do you currently do best? Which is the one you will need to work hardest to improve?

5. What adaptations would you need to make in the feedback you offer students with different types of assessment—for example, short quizzes compared to essays, compositions, demonstrations, projects, or reports?

6. Can you imagine instances where it will be more challenging to offer students feedback that adequately addresses all three essential questions?

5 FEEDBACK TO PARENTS AND FAMILIES

In most instances, we give feedback to learners, and in the case of instructional feedback in schools, we give feedback to students. But there is another important group of stakeholders in the instructional equation, and that is parents and families. We mention parents *and* families because some families include primary caregivers other than parents—for example, grandparents, aunts and uncles, and even older siblings. For the sake of simplicity, in this chapter we will simply refer to those who provide care and support to children as "parents," acknowledging that there are a variety of ways that such support is realized.

THE "LEARNING TEAM"

Most parents are vitally interested in the academic success of their children. In fact, some parents may actually be too interested at times. For the most part, however, parents can be thought of as part of a "learning team" working toward the school success of their child and your student.

Parents can be thought of as part of a "learning team" working toward the school success of their child and your student.

Some parents have many resources to bring to that effort, some have fewer, and, sadly, some have next to none. Single parents, parents struggling economically just to get by, and parents working through personal or family issues simply may be unable to offer much help. But that should never be taken to mean that they aren't deeply concerned about their child's welfare and learning progress.

It is also important to keep in mind that what you are teaching might be well beyond the capabilities of many parents. For example, few parents will recall how to diagram a sentence, even though they learned that skill in middle school. Likewise, most parents won't remember how to solve quadratic equations, even if they took an algebra class in high school. Nevertheless, it is up to you as a teacher to enlist, develop, guide, and maintain whatever level of support parents are able to provide. In most cases, this is easier to do at the elementary level than in the later years, but it's still something you should aspire to.

Nevertheless, it is up to you as a teacher to enlist, develop, guide, and maintain whatever level of support parents are able to provide.

https://bit.ly/
3DGiQGT
To read a QR
code, you
must have a
smartphone
or tablet with
a camera. We
recommend
that you
download
a QR code
reader app
that is made
specifically for
your phone or
tablet brand.

There are many good resources on developing positive and productive relationships with parents (see, for example, the QR code on this page). Our concern here, however, is providing feedback to parents about their child's learning progress. So the questions for us become "What should that feedback look like?"; "How should it be delivered?"; and "How can we use feedback to develop and maintain strong and supportive relationships with parents?"

Families are a part of a child's learning team.

Source: istock.com/SDI Productions

WHAT SHOULD FEEDBACK TO PARENTS LOOK LIKE?

We believe feedback to parents should look much like it does for students, with a few slight twists. After all, parents are not the learners; the students are.

What Are the Learning Goals?

To begin, parents need to know specifically what you are working on with their child in terms of academic growth and achievement. This can be done in a fairly straightforward manner through conversations with parents, as shown in the following examples:

Feedback to parents should look much like it does for students, with a few slight twists.

- "We're working on developing students' skills for problem solving in mathematics. In particular, we are interested in helping students to take what we call 'word problems' that describe practical situations involving mathematics, and then to figure out what mathematics is needed to come up with an answer. Let me give you an example . . ."

- "We're working on what is called 'sentence structure.' I'm showing the students different kinds of sentences and clauses that they can use to get more variety in their writing. Here's an example that we were working on today . . ."

- "I'm introducing the idea of states of energy. Now, there are a variety of ways to look at this. What we've done so far . . ."

It's always good to give an example of what you mean. Many parents may be unfamiliar with the names we attach to particular concepts and skills, but are reluctant to ask for a more detailed explanation. Instead, they simply nod knowingly, just to be polite, and invite you to go on, even when they have no idea what you are talking about.

What Has Your Child Learned Well, and What Are the Difficulties?

After laying out your current learning goals—regardless of whether you call them objectives, targets, trajectories, learning aims, or competencies—parents will want to know how their child is doing. This can be tough, especially if a child is struggling. Our advice is always to be honest, but be kind and positive with your honesty.

Your focus should be to describe where their child is "right now." But you also want to emphasize that struggle is not unusual, that it is always temporary, and that our shared mission is to ensure their child's timely improvement. Here are some examples:

Be honest, but be kind and positive with your honesty.

- "As you know, Maria is a great reader, and a fast one, too. But occasionally, especially when working on mathematics word problems, it would be helpful if she just slowed down a little bit. She is so eager to get the problem done that sometimes she assumes what is going on rather than reading the problem carefully. So that's what we're working on. Here's an example of what I would like her to do . . ."

- "Jack is really good at using colorful and descriptive language. He always surprises me with the words he chooses. What we're trying to do is to get him to vary the types of sentences he chooses. Jack tends to rely on only subject/verb/modifier types of sentences. Let me show you what I mean from his most recent essay . . ."

- "Esteban struggled a bit with our last unit on the periodic table. It seemed he wasn't all that excited about it. But now, in our current energy unit, he seems much more engaged. Maybe you could ask him about that. We want to be sure he stays on track for the Advanced Placement exam. I know it's a ways off, but better to stay on top of things . . ."

What's Next, and How Can Parents Help?

This is probably the most difficult and most delicate step in the feedback process. Some parents will be very forthcoming and will immediately ask you, "What can we do to help?" Others will be more timid and simply smile, nod, look concerned, and not say much. The question you have to consider is "How can I find out how much they are willing to participate and what they believe their contribution should be?"

We know, for example, that parents of young children are often concerned about how their child is progressing in reading. We also know that home influence can be very important in developing early literacy skills. So encouraging parents to read to their child at home, have the child read along, and then eventually ask the child to read books to them can be an important part of this process. An easy way to enlist the parents' help in this process is simply to ask directly about home reading. For example, you might ask, "Is reading to Elodie at home something you enjoy? Does he seem to enjoy it, too? Is reading together part of your regular home activities? If you like, I can make some suggestions." The point is, you can't know if you don't ask! Finding out what is going on at home, and making suggestions to parents about how they can participate in their child's learning, can add greatly to the success you see in children at school.

Finding out what is going on at home, and making suggestions to parents about how they can participate in their child's learning, can add greatly to the success you see in children at school.

One topic that is likely to come up in talking with parents, especially those with children at the secondary level, is the issue of homework. Under some conditions, and especially when homework assignments are specifically designed to engage students in conversations with parents (e.g., "Ask your parents what they remember about . . ."), homework can serve as a form of feedback. Encouraging elementary students to discuss homework assignments with their parents can help inform parents about learning goals and the kinds of activities in which students are engaging.

Research on homework shows, however, that its effectiveness varies depending on the grade level of students and both the purpose and the nature of the assignment (Cooper, 2007; Cooper et al., 2006). What's clear in the research is that there is little benefit in "homework for homework's sake." Every homework assignment should have a clear purpose. And if parents have a role in any homework assignment, that role should be made clear. It may be to ensure students work on their own, to check to make sure the assignment is complete, to provide assistance if asked, to review for correctness, or simply to make sure it's in the backpack in the morning. In some cases, parents may ask teachers for a different homework assignment for their children. For example, the son of one of this book's authors was excellent at math, so kindergarten homework asking him to "color 11 cows" felt like punishment. After his parents shared this with the teacher, Evan was allowed to work on sudoku puzzles instead. Opening channels of communication with the parents is of key importance to student success.

HOW SHOULD FEEDBACK BE DELIVERED?

The timeliness of feedback to parents can be critically important. Especially when a student is experiencing learning difficulties or consistently acting out or misbehaving, it's best to intervene early and enlist family members as your helpers.

Feedback should always be delivered to parents in a way that helps them to understand that you are "on their child's side."

Feedback should always be delivered to parents in a way that helps them to understand that you are "on their child's side." This is true regardless of whether that interaction with parents occurs in a parent–teacher conference, an email message, a phone call, or even a casual conversation. An easy way to do that is to follow a simple, four-step process we have outlined elsewhere (see Guskey, 2019). Specifically, in that feedback you should:

1. *Always begin with something positive.* Your comments to parents should first point out what their child does well and what successes they have had.

2. *Identify what specific aspects of their child's performance need to improve.* Parents need to know precisely what difficulties (if any) their child is experiencing so they know where improvement efforts should be targeted.

3. *Offer specific guidance and direction for making improvements.* Parents also want guidance from teachers about what steps they can take to help their child improve and better meet the learning expectations for the subject area or class.

4. *Express confidence in their child's ability to succeed.* Probably most important, parents need to know that you believe in their child, are on their side, see value in their child's work, and are confident their child can achieve whatever learning goals are set.

For example, in a phone conversation with parents about a particular student's performance in a high school language arts class, Mr. MacTavish explained:

> "In our recent unit of poetry, Chris wrote several excellent haiku poems that showed amazing creativity. A haiku is a traditional Japanese form of poetry that consists of only three lines and usually only 17 syllables, often focusing on images from nature. But he often neglects homework assignments and comes to class unprepared. You might ask him about his homework each evening and ensure he has a quiet place at home to work on preparing for the next day's class. I'm sure if he prepares a bit better, Chris will do very well in class."

This brief explanation showed that Mr. MacTavish knew Chris and was familiar with his work, recognized what Chris had done well, noted areas for improvement and offered specific suggestions, and expressed confidence that Chris could learn excellently. What parent would not feel good about their child's prospects for success and have confidence in their child's teacher after such a conversation?

PARENT–TEACHER CONFERENCES

Parent–teacher conferences, which have different names in different countries, are perhaps the most common way of presenting feedback to parents. Many schools also have open-house meetings and "back to school" nights that usually occur at the beginning of the school year. But those generally serve to introduce parents to teachers and lay out what the year will look like. Parent–teacher conferences are usually when the first true feedback occurs. As such, they represent an extremely important venue for communication with parents.

We've participated in parent–teacher conferences both as teachers and as parents, and we have some suggestions on how you can make them successful and productive. First and foremost, never underestimate the importance of parent–teacher conferences.

Never underestimate the importance of parent–teacher conferences.

From a feedback perspective, they represent what typically will be your first opportunity to let parents know how their child is doing and how they can help ensure progress. Second, parent–teacher conferences give parents the chance to get to know you. Because their child will likely spend time with you every school day, parents want to know what you are like as a person and as a professional. And third, parent–teacher conferences give you the opportunity to communicate with a broad audience of stakeholders. The parents of your students are likely to know board members or may themselves be members of the school board. They know principals, assistant principals, counselors, secretaries, and other important members of the school community. When you talk with your students' parents, you are communicating with a much larger audience of education stakeholders than you might imagine.

If you feel a bit anxious about upcoming parent–teacher conferences, we can assure you that parents are just as anxious. They know that your impression of them could potentially influence future interactions you have with their child. So, like you, they want to ensure the impression you have of them is just as positive as the impression you hope they have of you. We are reminded of the words of a great teacher educator, Joseph Zelnick, who in explaining to aspiring teachers the importance of parent–conferences would stress: "You have to remember, these are the very best children these people have."

MAKING THE MOST OF PARENT–TEACHER CONFERENCES

There is a wealth of resources to consult on the topic of parent–teacher conferences. One example we have found especially helpful is at the QR code on this page. But from the perspective of feedback to parents, here are several recommendations for ensuring the success of parent–teacher conferences:

https://bit.ly/
3BNlmc3

To begin, in planning parent–teacher conferences, make sure you schedule enough time so you're not rushing parents out the door. But also be sure that parents understand the schedule and the need to respect the time promised to other parents.

Next, make sure parents feel welcome when they arrive. If they must wait in the hallway until their scheduled conference appointment, be sure to have comfortable chairs available for them and perhaps post a sign asking them to knock on the door when it is time for their conference. This will also help you to conclude a conference that may be getting overextended.

In addition, know who the parents are and how to pronounce their names. Know in advance if the parents you are about to meet speak English, and if they don't, arrange for someone to translate. The same is true for parents with any form of disability. It's *your* job to make sure any needed accommodations are provided so parents feel comfortable.

At an initial meeting, always address parents more formally as Mr. and Ms., unless they ask you to do otherwise. *You* should initiate the greeting with a smile and ask them to please come in. In addition, be sure to have adult-sized chairs available for them. There is nothing more uncomfortable than asking an adult to sit in a chair designed for a six-year-old. Having snacks to offer also goes a long way, even if no one takes them, because it shows you are thinking about their needs.

A big part of communicating the right message is to make sure the seating arrangements show you are all on the same team. In other words, don't sit behind your desk with the parents in front of you. Having a round table where you can lay out the student's work and go over specific examples, while sitting together, sends a much better message.

As we mentioned earlier, always start the conference by saying something positive about their child. Let parents know that you know their child, you like having their child in your class, and you have their child's best interests at heart. Be sure to prepare what you are going to say to break the ice and let the parents know that you truly care about their child's well-being. Conversations with colleagues who have had their child in previous classes can often be helpful in this regard.

Finally, when parents come to see you, be sure you are ready for them. You should be up to date with their child's progress and ready to show examples of the things you want to talk about. Be organized, thorough, and thoughtful in what you say and in how you say it.

Be organized, thorough, and thoughtful in what you say and in how you say it.

Make a point of talking about *only* their child and avoid making comparisons to other children, even if parents ask. Under no conditions should you say anything negative about any other child or another teacher. Be sure to watch your body language to ensure it communicates that you are open to them and interested in what they have to say. And try to avoid education-speak. For example, most parents won't know what formative assessment or an IEP is.

RECOMMENDATIONS FOR BETTER PRACTICE

Let's review these recommendations:

1. *Be ready for all your conferences.* Have materials organized and ready to go. Allow enough time, but not too much time.

2. *Be welcoming.* Provide chairs and maybe a note on the door to knock when parents arrive.

3. *Know who's coming to see you.* Do you need a translator, either for a spoken language or for ASL (American Sign Language)? Are there accessibility issues?

4. *Have a place for the conference to occur* with chairs that are usable for bigger people and where you can sit at a round table or on the same side of a table.

5. *Start positive.* Let parents know that you know their child and have their child's best interests at heart.

6. *Let parents know what you are currently working on and what the goals are.* Avoid educational jargon or, if needed, explain any terms they may not know.

7. *Describe how their child is doing.* Outline both strengths and weaknesses. Be prepared to show examples to illustrate your points. Avoid making comparisons to other children in the class, even indirectly. You also want to avoid statements such as "Tommy is the best math student I have this year."

8. *Talk about upcoming lessons and learning goals*, what their child is working on, and how they can help.

9. *Ask parents* if they have questions.

10. *Really listen.* Parents may know best, after all.

11. *Conclude* with how you are going to stay in touch.

STUDENT-LED CONFERENCES

A great alternative to the traditional parent–teacher conference is to have the student join in and actually take a lead role in conducting the conference. In student-led conferences, students typically lead parents through a portfolio of their work, noting the purpose of different examples of their performance, describing what they learned well and have mastered, and explaining where they need to work a bit harder or make additional effort. As a teacher, you become an observer and a resource available to answer any questions that might arise.

https://edut
.to/3BPe20a.

Student-led conferences can take a variety of forms and offer a number of important benefits, especially in helping students develop a greater sense of personal responsibility and agency for their performance in school. Although the details involved in setting up student-led conferences in your classroom are beyond the scope of our focus on feedback, there are several great resources available to you. One is the excellent book *Implementing Student-Led Conferences* by Jane Bailey and Thomas Guskey (2001). Another is the *Edutopia* blog; scan the QR code on this page to view the blog.

KEEPING IN TOUCH

Once you establish a relationship with parents, it's important to keep in touch with them. Technology offers a great way to do that. A quick email, text message, or phone call to parents to tell them about something great their child did in class or a particular learning success they achieved can make a parent's week. Also, letting parents know about learning difficulties that a student is having or behavior issues that seem to be developing can help resolve those difficulties early and prevent them from becoming major problems. It also sends the message to parents that you are on top of things.

Video conferences and online check-ins with students and parents is a great option to stay in touch.

Many teachers develop class websites that can bring parents, grandparents, and other caregivers up to date on what is happening in the class. On the website you can also include reminders about class projects and upcoming events, as well as provide contact information for the school and for you. Keeping the lines of communication open with parents is a great way to facilitate learning.

At the same time, if parents are unwilling or unable to be in touch with the school, it's the teacher's job to offer extra support to the students. Not all students have supportive and interested families, but all students deserve a chance at optimal learning and a supportive atmosphere.

Keeping the lines of communication open with parents is a great way to facilitate learning.

SUMMARY AND TAKEAWAYS

Parents are our allies in encouraging student learning. When they understand the learning goals, what their child has learned well and what difficulties their child may be experiencing, and what they can do to help, parents can be a great asset in learning. Providing parents with clear, understandable, and actionable feedback about their child's learning accomplishes precisely that.

Parent–teacher conferences, student-led conferences, and keeping in touch through phone calls, text messages, email, and class websites establish and maintain that critical line of communication. Although parents will vary in how able and willing they are to support their children's learning, most are willing to do what they can, when they know what to do.

When they understand the learning goals, what their child has learned well and what difficulties their child may be experiencing, and what they can do to help, parents can be a great asset in learning.

Feedback to parents should communicate that you care about their child. It should provide clear information on the learning goals, students' current learning status, and what needs to be done to improve. Parent–teacher conferences are an important venue for providing that feedback, and we discussed specific steps to follow to ensure success. The key is to open the lines of communication between school and home, provide specific guidance to parents as to how they can help their child, stress that you are partners in ensuring the success of their child, and maintain a positive, growth-oriented approach to learning.

If you are relatively new to teaching and nervous about upcoming parent–teacher conferences, you might want to seek advice from your colleagues. You might even consider practicing a time or two in mock conferences with your colleagues or friends. So long as you listen carefully to what parents have to say, are sensitive to their concerns, offer practical suggestions for how you can work together, and stress that you are partners in ensuring their child's welfare and success, you are sure to do well.

QUESTIONS TO CONSIDER

1. Organization and preparation are essential to providing quality feedback to parents. How do you prepare for a conference? What student work do you typically show to communicate their progress? What do you usually suggest parents can do to help?

2. Sometimes parents don't show up at conferences, and sometimes you might get as many as four parents showing up at once, especially in the case of blended families. You might get two moms or two dads. You might get grandparents. You might get a mom and a dad who are divorced but sharing custody. How can you prepare for whoever shows up at your classroom door?

3. How would you navigate a parent–teacher conference for a child who you are really concerned about, or who has presented serious behavioral, emotional, or social issues in the classroom?

4. Scheduling can be difficult as some parents work in the evening, or perhaps have other commitments. Also, some parents will want to have a long discussion, while others anticipate a cursory one. How can you make your schedule flexible in order to meet the needs of your students and their parents, and yet maintain a proper work–life balance?

6 GRADES AS FEEDBACK[1]

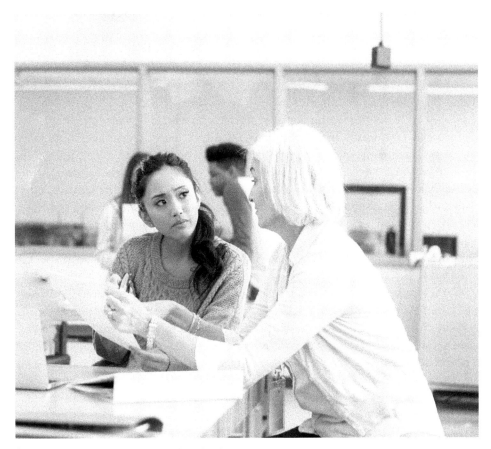

"There must be some mistake. I'm an A student."

Source: istock.com/SDI Productions

Nearly every day we read articles, newspaper editorials, and blogs telling us that grades are education's evil and malicious villain. Some authors say that grades stifle creativity, foster fear of failure, and weaken students' interest (Pulfrey et al., 2011). Others say that grades have a negative effect on students and reduce their engagement in learning

---

[1] This chapter is based on the paper "Can Grades Be an Effective Form of Feedback," presented at the annual meeting of the American Educational Research Association, San Diego, CA, April 2022.

(Poorthuis et al., 2015). This has caused some to suggest that we could significantly improve students' attitudes, interest in learning, and classroom learning environments by eliminating grades and going "gradeless" (Barnes, 2018; Burns & Frangiosa, 2021; Kohn, 1994, 1999; Spencer, 2017).

"PERHAPS, BUT . . ."

"Perhaps, but . . . I *have* to give grades. This isn't really an option for me. How do I handle having to give grades on at least some assignments, but still trying to promote learning as my primary goal?"

FLIPPING THE SCRIPT ON GRADING

Although grades don't exist in all schools in all countries, especially not at the primary level, they are a fact of teaching for most teachers. In addition, grades have important consequences for students. In schools throughout North America, grades are the primary criteria in determining students' promotion from one grade level to the next. They are the basis of school honor rolls and govern students' entry into advanced classes. At the secondary level, grades determine students' eligibility for extracurricular activities, especially interscholastic sports, and are a major factor considered in the college admission process. At the postsecondary level, grades are considered in granting financial aid and determine if students are permitted to continue in their education program. Although we could debate the appropriateness of using grades for these purposes, there is no debate that these consequences exist.

The importance attached to grades creates a tension with which educators have struggled for more than a century (see Brookhart, 2016). As teachers, we are advocates for our students. We want them all to do well. Nothing makes us happier than our students' success. But when we assign grades, we leave the role of advocates and become judges of our students. Now, to be sure, we are judging their work, not the students, and that is an important distinction. But it often feels like we are judging the students themselves. And students often take the marks they see at the top of their papers as statements about them as individuals.

But do grades have to be the terrible culprit that so many have made them out to be? Would getting rid of grades suddenly increase students' interest in learning and make our classrooms better places to learn? No strong research evidence indicates that to be the case. And even if we advocate for serious research looking into that question, the reality is that many teachers are required to give grades. So, the question is not simply "Should we give grades?" but rather "When we give grades, how can we do so in the most positive way?"

So, the question is not simply "Should we give grades?" but rather "When we give grades, how can we do so in the most positive way?"

The best approach to this issue might be to take a serious look at grades, try to identify the strengths and weaknesses of giving grades, and then imagine how we could modify grade giving to make it a more uniformly positive experience. For example, we know that students' feelings about grades and how grades affect them depend on the purpose and meaning attached to grades.

Interpretations also vary depending on how grades are determined, the level and background of the students involved, and the classroom learning conditions (Guskey, 2019). Furthermore, students' perceptions of grades and how students respond to grades depend on what grade they receive (Link & Guskey, 2019) and whether they believe the grading process is fair.

We know, too, that grades can be and often are misused. This occurs when teachers use grades to "reward" students for following academic and behavioral expectations, or to "punish" students for being irresponsible and not following directions. It also happens when grades are used for sorting purposes or are determined based on students' relative standing among classmates, a practice we call "grading on the curve." To grade on the curve, teachers first rank all students in a particular class according to some arbitrary measure of achievement (Brookhart et al., 2016). Then the top-ranked 10% or so get As, the next 20% or so get Bs, and so on. Grades assigned in this way serve no formative purpose whatsoever, but are strictly summative evaluations. They are a simple, shorthand way of saying, "This is where you ended up in this course in comparison to your classmates."

Because of the long history of these types of grading practices, many students and teachers see grades only as final, culminating, summative judgments of what students have achieved and can achieve. If a student receives a C on a major assessment in algebra, that's it. That portion of the course is over, and the grade is a C. There is no chance to improve that grade, and no further learning is expected to occur in that area of algebra for the foreseeable future. But does it have to be that way? Should it be?

Suppose we are talking about a grade of C on an essay written about a third of the way through a French II course. If that essay cannot be revised, and the grade is considered part of the student's final course grade, then again it is being used summatively. But could we improve that type of practice? Could we make practical changes that would actually serve to enhance learning and lead to greater learning success?

Our point here—and it is a serious one—is that although grades can serve as feedback on performance, they don't function that way at all when used summatively. As part of a summative course grade, that C one third of the way through French II offers no opportunity for improvement. Instead, it functions as an anchor on the student's final course grade, no matter how much more that student learns in French II throughout the rest of the academic term. It stifles motivation, diminishes self-confidence, and lessens students' effort, resulting in a subsequent loss of achievement. We need to turn that around.

Specifically, we need to use grades in much more enlightened ways. We need to implement grading policies and practices that help students view grades not summatively, as inalterable final judgments, but formatively, as temporary markers of their current level of performance. In this way, grades *can* be an effective form of feedback for students and *can* serve to enhance learning.

Students' feelings about grades and how grades affect them depend on the purpose and meaning attached to grades.

We need to use grades in much more enlightened ways. We need to implement grading policies and practices that help students view grades not summatively, as inalterable final judgments, but formatively, as temporary markers of their current level of performance. In this way, grades can be an effective form of feedback for students and can serve to enhance learning.

To guarantee their more productive use and avoid misuse, however, we need to be sure that students, along with their parents and families, understand that a given grade can be improved (with a few exceptions, such as end-of-year assessments). In addition, teachers at all levels need to develop and implement grading policies and practices that highlight the formative use of grades as feedback, while reducing their potentially negative connotations. We need to make grades work for us and for our students, rather than working against us.

We need to make grades work for us and for our students, rather than working against us.

Before talking about how to make grades work in the best possible way, however, let us offer a general rule of thumb given our current context. This rule stems from our recognition of the long- and well-established tradition of grades being used as summative judgments, our understanding of students' and families' perceptions of grades based on that tradition, and our acknowledgment of how difficult it will be to alter those perceptions quickly and efficiently.

Our rule of thumb is this: If you don't have to assign grades, even temporary ones, it is best not to do so.

Our rule of thumb is this: If you don't have to assign grades, even temporary ones, it is best not to do so. Instead, provide information about how to improve directly to the student. If grades are required, then consider what follows as a way to ensure grades yield the best possible result.

WHAT ARE GRADES?

When it comes to their meaning, grades are simply labels assigned to different levels or categories of student performance. They identify how well students did on a particular task or learning goal. These labels can be letters, numbers, words, symbols, or even emojis (see Figure 6.1). As we described earlier in this chapter, they can be used in a formative fashion, indicating where students currently stand in their learning. Knowing where you are in your learning is a critical component of feedback and subsequent improvement in learning.

FIGURE 6.1 ■ Labels for Different Categories of Student Performance

Letters	Numerals	Descriptors	Emojis
A	4	Exemplary	😎
B	3	Proficient	🙂
C	2	Developing	😕
D	1	Struggling	😔
F	0	No Evidence	🙁

Source: emoji icons from istock.com/Iefym Turkin

As discussed in earlier chapters, feedback is the "second part" of teaching. The first part involves teachers' initial instruction and student activities to impart new knowledge and skills, combined with assessment procedures to evaluate students' understanding and level of mastery. The feedback part relates to three major questions that we revised:

1. What are the learning goals?

2. What have I learned?

3. What's next?

In this way, feedback operates much like a global positioning system (GPS) for travelers. In using a GPS, travelers first identify their destination ("What are the learning goals?"). The GPS then determines the travelers' current location ("What have I learned?") and plots a route from there to the intended destination ("What's next?"). The feedback teachers offer to students similarly helps them navigate the learning route from where they are currently to achieving the final learning goals.

Grades relate to the second of these three questions—specifically, "What have I learned?" or "How well did I perform on this task?" (see the discussion in Chapter 2 on learning versus performance distinction). Grades can provide a summary of what progress students currently have made toward their goals. They can indicate the current level of achievement, where students are on their learning path, and how near to or far from their destination they are—that is, where students are in relation to achieving the learning goal. The important question is "How can we change students' perceptions of grades as summative judgments to make sure they function well as feedback?"

MAKING GRADES FUNCTION EFFECTIVELY AS FEEDBACK

In situations when we do give grades, we must ensure the grades we assign help students in their learning by functioning as effective feedback. To do that, the grades we assign must meet four necessary conditions. These conditions not only allow grades to serve important formative purposes; they also help remove the negative consequences that typically accompany the misuse of grades.

Grades reflect not who you are as a learner, but where you are in your learning journey.

1. Grades Should Be Assigned to Performance, Not to Students

As early on as possible, we need to stress to students and their parents/families that grades reflect not *who* you are as a learner, but *where* you are in your learning journey.

We also have to emphasize that grades *never* describe a student's capabilities or learning potential. Instead, grades are simply an indication of how near to or far from reaching specific learning goals students are.

Many times, students see grades as a reflection of their talent, skills, or abilities. Seen this way, grades can become personal labels that students assign to themselves and can be difficult to change. There's nothing sadder than a teacher hearing a student say, "I'm just a C student."

When accompanied by guidance on how to do better, grades can provide an important starting point for making those improvements.

But when students, parents, and families see grades as a reflection of current performance only, they recognize that knowing where you are is essential for making improvement. As teachers, our evaluations of students' performance can help students become more thoughtful evaluators of their own work. After all, a grade, number, or symbol offers only a shorthand description of where students are, and additional information is needed to direct progress. When accompanied by guidance on how to do better, grades can provide an important starting point for making those improvements.

"IF ONLY . . ."

One of our favorite stories about unfair grading practice comes from a highly accomplished education professor:

"If only I had bowled more poorly, I would have graduated summa cum laude. The only grade I had as an undergraduate that wasn't an A was in physical education in a bowling class. I had attended every class, worked as hard as I could, and thought I had done well. But it turns out that in order to get an A, you had to bowl better on your last game than you had done at the beginning of the course. Always trying to do my best, I had a pretty good game at the start of the course. Had I known that improving was the key to an A, I would have bowled much more poorly on that first game and gotten the A easily. But the instructor never told us that! That was almost a half century ago, and it still aggravates me to no end."

"If only I had bowled more poorly . . ."
Source: istock.com/recep-bg

2. Grades Should Be Criterion-Based, Not Norm-Based

In some classes, teachers assign grades based on how students' performance compares to their classmates. As we described earlier in this chapter, we call this "norm-based" or "ego-involving" grading. At upper grade levels and in college-level classes, we refer to this as "grading on the curve." In norm-based grading, a grade of C doesn't mean you are at step three in a five-step process to mastery. Instead, it means your performance ranks you in the middle of the class and is "average" in comparison to your classmates.

Norm-based grading results in a number of negative consequences (see Guskey & Brookhart, 2019). First, it tells students nothing about what they have learned or are able to do. Students who receive high grades might have performed quite poorly, just less poorly than their classmates. Second, it makes the classroom environment highly competitive, since students must compete against one another for the few high grades given by the teacher. Third, it discourages any type of student collaboration, because helping others threatens students' own chances for success. In these classrooms, doing well does not mean learning excellently; it means outdoing your classmates. And fourth, norm-based grading weakens student–teacher relationships, since teachers offering individualized support to students may be seen as showing favoritism and interfering with the competition (Guskey, 2000).

The alternative to norm-based grading is called "criterion-based" or "task-involving" grading. It describes how well students have performed in relation to specific learning goals. Using this method of grading, students are evaluated on clearly defined performance expectations and have no relation to the performance of other students. Because students compete against learning goals and not each other, criterion-based grading encourages student collaboration. Helping classmates succeed actually serves to enhance students' success. It also puts teachers and students on the same side, working together to master the learning goals. The direct meaning of criterion-based grades allows them to serve well the communication purposes for which grades are intended.

Most teachers use a criterion-referenced approach to grading rather than a norm-referenced approach, especially at lower grade levels. But often those who do wonder, "Gee, am I giving too many As?" But if the criteria are clear, you aren't "giving" anything; the students are earning their grades. In addition, if your learning goals are sufficiently rigorous and you are happy with them, why wouldn't you want *all* of your students to achieve those goals?

CRITICAL MISINTERPRETATIONS

Failure to recognize important differences in the consequences of norm-based versus criterion-based grades has led to critical misinterpretations of studies on the impact of grades. A prime example is the 1988 study by Ruth Butler, frequently cited by critics of grades to show the supposed detrimental effects of grades on students' interest and motivation. In her study, Butler compared the impact of three feedback conditions on fifth- and sixth-grade students. One group of students received only grades as feedback on a learning task, another group received only comments, and a third group received both grades and comments. Results showed that students' interest and performance were generally higher after receiving comments than after receiving grades alone or grades with comments.

What most of the critics who cite this study fail to mention is that the grades assigned by teachers in Butler's (1988) study were norm-based, ego-involving grades that communicated *nothing* about what students had learned. They were numbers ranging from 40 to 99 based on students' relative standing among classmates. The comments teachers provided, however, were criterion-based, task-involving comments that offered students information about their performance on the learning task *and* gave direction for improvement.

In addition, the results of Butler's study were not consistent. The effects were true *only* for students ranked in the bottom 25% of their class—that is, students who received the lowest grades. Students ranked in the top 25% of their class who received high grades maintained their high interest and motivation. In other words, the influence of grades on motivation varied depending on the grade students received. The study did not consider the effects on the 50% of students who ranked in the middle of their class (Guskey, 2019).

A more recent study comparing grades and comments in which teachers assigned criterion-based, task-involving grades found very different results. Emma Smith and Stephen Gorard (2005) compared four groups of seventh-grade students who were given different forms of feedback. One group received "enhanced formative feedback" on their work for one year, but no marks or grades. The other three groups were given marks and grades with minimal comments. Results showed that progress in the comment-only group was "substantially inferior" to that of the other three groups and unpopular with the students as well.

Smith and Gorard (2005) noted they were not able to analyze the quality of the comments students received because it was beyond the scope of their study. Still, their investigation made clear that the effects of feedback given to students depend more on its *quality* and *substance* than on its form or structure—that is, grades versus comments. As Hattie and Timperley (2007) emphasize, the *quality*, *nature*, and *content* of the feedback matter most.

The effects of feedback given to students depend more on its quality and substance than on its form or structure

In our own studies we have repeatedly found that college students who received grades in addition to comments performed less well on revisions, compared to those who didn't receive grades on their initial drafts. This is especially true for higher- and lower-scoring students. That is, a student who received a preliminary grade of A tended to spend significantly less time on revisions, compared to a peer who didn't see their grade. We suspect this is because, in their way of thinking, the goal is not necessarily to learn well or to master a particular subject but, rather, to earn a high grade. Having accomplished that goal, they feel there is no need to do anything more. The low scorers didn't improve more for different reasons. These students felt ashamed, guilty, and sad, and as a result devoted fewer resources to revisions. One student described the comments versus grades difference as "Comments tell you what to do, and grades tell you how much you need to do. I got a B and was happy with it. So I moved two words around and left." Having received the grade she wanted, this particular student seemed inclined to preserve her time and resource investment, not work on revisions. But as educators, isn't our goal to have students move as far as they can go in their performance?

In other words, if there is an opportunity to revise, grades should be omitted.

In other words, if there is an opportunity to revise, grades should be omitted.

3. Grades Should Be Temporary

A student's level of performance is never permanent. As students continue to study, practice, and correct learning errors, their understanding gets better, and their performance improves.

To accurately describe how well students have learned, grades should never be permanent but should reflect students' current performance level.

To accurately describe how well students have learned, grades should never be permanent but should reflect students' current performance level.

When we help students understand that grades are temporary, they recognize that assessments don't mean the end of learning. Instead, assessment results and the grades that accompany them describe where students currently are in their journey to mastery. Achieving less than mastery doesn't mean you can't make it; it only means that you haven't made it *yet*, and there's more to do.

Admittedly, as teachers we must assign grades at a particular point in time. But as time goes on and students' performance improves, we must be willing to change grades in order to reflect that improvement.

Knowing where students were at an earlier point in time tells us nothing about where they are now. This temporary quality of grades should also make us question the process of averaging, which combines evidence from the past with current evidence. A poor early grade can permanently pull a student's ultimate grade down if we rely on simple averaging. Averaging often yields an inaccurate depiction of what students have actually achieved. Instead, we must be willing to replace past evidence with current evidence in order to ensure grades are accurate and valid.

As time goes on and students' performance improves, we must be willing to change grades in order to reflect that improvement.

4. Grades Should Be Accompanied by Guidance and Opportunity for Improvement

Although it's important for us to indicate to students where they are in their learning journey, students also need to know what to do to reach their destination. Students need guidance and direction on how to make better progress, reach the goals, and achieve success. This is true of all forms of feedback.

Students need guidance and direction on how to make better progress, reach the goals, and achieve success.

Grades at best offer only a general, holistic reflection of students' current level of performance. They don't provide the detailed information students need to identify their specific learning strengths and difficulties, or the guidance and direction students need to improve their learning. Only when grades are accompanied by specific guidance for improvement can they become a valuable aspect of effective feedback.

SUMMARY AND TAKEAWAYS

Grades have historically been used to present a summary statement of where a student stands with regard to achievement in a given subject. This chapter has looked at how grades can be used in a more formative fashion, one that does not seek to place a stamp on

Grades should never be the only information about learning that we offer students, parents, and families.

a student at a given point in time, but rather indicates where a student is currently in their learning journey, and how that student might progress.

Students need honest information from us as teachers about the quality and adequacy of their performance in school. Parents/families need to know how well their children are doing and whether or not grade-level or course expectations are being met. However, grades should never be the *only* information about learning that we offer students, parents, and families.

When we combine grades with guidance to students, parents, and families on how improvements can be made, they become a valuable tool in facilitating students' learning success and an effective form of feedback. However, in situations in which students have the opportunity to improve their work, grades have limited instructional value.

In situations in which students have the opportunity to improve their work, grades have little instructional value.

As a student getting formative feedback once noted: "I always hated grades because they don't tell you anything. I'm sitting there thinking this is great; I can fix anything I messed up on. I can make it better . . . So I don't think grades or praise would be good. Just comments, tell me what I did wrong, where I could change it. Just comments and error marks."

QUESTIONS TO CONSIDER

1. What would happen if your school simply eliminated grades completely? What would the consequences be?

2. How do your students typically respond to the grades they get?

3. What were *your* best and worst experiences in receiving grades when you were a student? (Perhaps sharing such stories would be a fun and productive activity with your fellow teachers.)

4. What kinds of comments can you provide to a student whose performance on an assignment or assessment is in the D to F range?

5. Can you think of cases in which comments alone would have a negative effect on students' motivation for learning and their perceptions of themselves as learners?

7 EFFICIENCY AND EFFECTIVENESS IN FEEDBACK

For most of us who chose education as a profession, teaching is a lifestyle more than a career. We are always thinking about how we can improve the lives of our students. If we see something clever on television, on the internet, or in a book, we think, "I could use that." It's only natural.

The authors of this book often go to instructional programs (museums, tours, adult classes, etc.) for two reasons. First, if you are going to teach, you should never stop being a learner. And second, it's helpful to see how people give feedback in nontraditional instructional settings. Teachers might be in the classroom for just 6 hours each day, but in their hearts, they are teachers 24/7.

If you are going to teach, you should never stop being a learner.

At the same time, teachers also need to carve out time away from their role as teachers. They need to decompress, spend time with family, and explore their own personal and professional development. To do that, they must *have* the time and know how to use that time well. So let's consider how to be efficient, as well as effective, with feedback.

Teachers need time to explore their personal goals and aspirations.

Source: Photo by Sergey Lipnevich.

To begin, let's review what feedback is. In Chapter 4, we described how instructional feedback provides information with regard to three important questions:

1. What are the learning goals?

2. What have I learned?

3. What's next?

Any information that is based on some kind of performance and helps the learner improve is feedback.

But what if a particular form of feedback addressed only one or two of those questions? Would it still be considered feedback? We believe it would. From our perspective, any information that is based on some kind of performance and helps the learner improve is feedback.

In this chapter, we explore feedback options that only make the learning goals clearer to the learner, and other feedback that addresses only what one has learned. Although these may not always be *as effective* as giving more extensive personal feedback, they are still effective forms of feedback. We recognize that several of the options presented here are less than ideal. Still, it isn't always possible to do everything for everyone all the time. We begin by looking at a critical element of feedback: self-assessment in feedback, or "self-feedback."

SELF-FEEDBACK

When we completed the first draft of this chapter, we reread it and made changes. In other words, we engaged in the process of self-feedback. Not every sentence was perfect. In some cases, entire sections needed to be revised. When that revision was completed, we sent it to our editor who provided additional feedback, known as "peer feedback," which we address in the next section.

The ability to be self-reflective is one of the key competencies of becoming a mature learner and engaging in lifelong learning.

Self-feedback occurs when learners reflect on work they have done and ask themselves how it can be improved and how they can do things differently in the future. The ability to be self-reflective is one of the key competencies of becoming a mature learner and engaging in lifelong learning.

Self-feedback begins with the motivation or encouragement to look critically at what one tried to do. Such feedback doesn't have to be elaborate. Take this simple elementary-level math problem:

Rhonda has twelve apples. She gives four apples to Mark and eats one herself. How many apples does Rhonda have left?

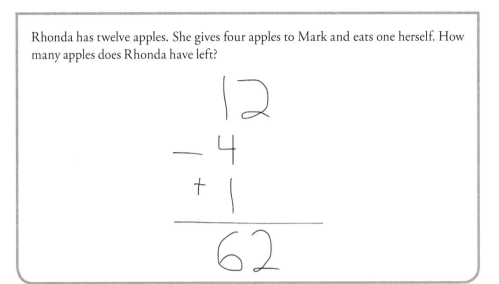

In this math problem, the student got some things right, but also made some rather critical mistakes, coming up with a final answer of 62, which is clearly wrong. A crucial math skill we want students to develop is the ability to make a general estimate of what the answer *ought* to be. Although there are some mechanics this student needs to work out, an important step forward would be the ability to see that this answer is not within the realm of possibility. That would be an example of self-feedback. Another crucial step would be for the student to say, "If the answer is not 62, where did I go wrong?"

At a more advanced level, imagine a student writing a persuasive essay to convince the reader of a particular point of view. A good way to engage in self-feedback on one's work on such an essay is to read what has been written from the perspective of the intended reader—in other words, to leave the "writer role" and adopt the "reader role." We could encourage a high school student to adopt the view of someone reading their work for the first time and ask, "Would I be convinced by this essay? What are the strong points and weak points? How could I make a more persuasive case?"

Self-feedback often occurs naturally. Anytime we say, "OK, this comment makes sense and this one doesn't, we are generating self-feedback. It also develops and evolves as students encounter feedback from teachers and peers. To develop this skill, however, students need a lot of practice. It's especially helpful if that practice is scaffolded. That is, begin with greater structure, and then gradually lessen or withdraw the structure. It is helpful, for example, to initially provide some of the aspects of good feedback to students, but then have them develop other aspects on their own.

PEER FEEDBACK

Peer feedback involves having students provide feedback on each other's work. This is often done reciprocally in pairs, but more than two students may be involved. In some cases, the feedback is given and received anonymously. Much of the research in this area involves writing and focuses on the higher education level. However, there is also work

https://bit.ly/
3BsBy2a

showing that peer feedback can be effective at the high school level and even at the elementary level (Andrade et al., 2019).

Peer feedback offers a number of important advantages. First, it gets feedback to students in a highly efficient fashion. In many instances, teachers are not directly involved in the process. Second, peer feedback holds the potential for positive social interactions (potentially negative interactions are described next). Third, peer feedback provides the scaffolded opportunity to develop the self-feedback skills described earlier. The ego involved in looking at one's own work can make areas for improvement difficult to see. Egos are mostly removed, however, when students are reviewing the work of others. See this video clip, for example, at the QR code on this page. In addition, peer feedback partners are seeing this work with fresh eyes. In this way, peer feedback can serve as a rehearsal of the process students need to effectively review their own work.

Peer feedback can be a powerful and efficient form of feedback.

Source: istock.com/kali9

In this way, peer feedback can serve as a rehearsal of the process students need to effectively review their own work.

Several important drawbacks and pitfalls to peer feedback also need to be kept in mind. Especially with younger students, peer feedback must be approached carefully and with substantial guidance, particularly when beginning this process in your classroom. One of the biggest problems with peer feedback when younger students are involved is that the feedback may not be accurate. In addition, it may not be kind or instructive.

As the teacher, you have to determine whether or not the climate in your classroom is amenable to engaging students in peer feedback.

There are specific things teachers can do to make their class more receptive to peer feedback activities. The appropriateness of these activities varies, of course, according to the age of students and the type of material they are reviewing. Sometimes it can be helpful to include specific prompts. For example, many teachers offer sentence stems or sample questions that students will extend when offering peer feedback.

Clarify	Am I reading this correctly?
Appreciate	What I think works really well is . . .
Think	Have you considered . . . ?
	Have you thought about . . . ?
Suggest	This part may work better if you . . .

We've listed some sites in the QR codes on this page for advice on peer feedback. In addition, here are a few general guidelines:

- Pair your students carefully. Do they get along well? How will they work with each other?

- Review the feedback before the recipient gets it.

- Use a rubric to guide peers in providing feedback. If you don't use a specific rubric, be sure to provide clear instructions on the types of things you want peers to comment on. For example, should they be looking for grammar and spelling issues, or are they providing a response to the overall ideas presented in the work?

- Emphasize kindness, helpfulness, and positivity!

These are just two websites we have found to be helpful. It's easy to search out more:

https://bit.ly/3Um2zwC   https://edut.to/3QVQyLu

DIGITAL/ELECTRONIC FEEDBACK

Digital or electronic feedback is an area that is developing rapidly. One particularly exciting aspect involves providing feedback on essays using computer programs. What can be accomplished electronically in terms of feedback on an essay is remarkable.

There are several types of electronic resources that we have found particularly helpful. Readability formulas found on the internet sort out text fairly well in terms of its sophistication and grade-level appropriateness. The spelling and grammar checkers built into word processors and cloud tools catch most spelling and grammar miscues. Programs that combine these two tools do a good job of providing feedback that can help students.

Other programs now available are even more sophisticated. In the box on collocations that follows, you will see an interesting example of what is called "natural language" in processing human speech and writing. Although nothing can replace a trained reader of prose when it comes to providing effective feedback, a high-quality computer program can augment our work and remove a lot of the drudgery involved in providing feedback on grammar and spelling. It's worth exploring!

CALLING ALL COLLOCATIONS

Collocations are two or more words that appear frequently in the English language or any language. For example, we see *powerful computers*, but not *strong computers*. We also see *strong tea*, but not *powerful tea*. Programs that do computer-based marking of essays often use the concept of collocations when marking essays.

The scores given by a computer and a person correlate as strongly as the scores given by two humans.

Research studies show that a computer-scored essay provides the same kinds of scores that humans do (Hussein et al., 2019). The scores given by a computer and a person correlate as strongly as the scores given by two humans. So allowing a computer to do the "grunt" work of providing feedback on grammar and spelling, and perhaps even improving sentence structure, might be appealing to you.

https://bit.ly/3BT2HN3.

Another potentially useful form of feedback is provided via video in what is called "screencasting." The advantage of screencasting feedback is it allows teachers to talk to students, complete with video; verbally point out issues of concern; and make specific suggestions for improvement. The QR code on this page provides a link to a site that talks about this approach.

Teachers can also provide students with automated feedback based on their responses to multiple-choice questions. Imagine a typical science multiple-choice assessment with items to which students' responses are either correct or incorrect. Teachers can program the feedback delivery platform to provide mini instructional episodes for each answer. That is, if a student selects option b, they will see an explanation as to why this answer is correct or incorrect. Students can click on every response and receive a clarification as to why each of the options either works or doesn't.

FEEDBACK THAT CLARIFIES
"WHAT ARE THE LEARNING GOALS?"

We have discussed three basic questions that feedback addresses. First, what are the learning goals? A learning goal might be "The student can produce an accurate and thorough lab report." Although at first glance this may appear to be a fairly clear goal/objective/achievement target, it isn't very specific. It doesn't provide any details about what should and should not be in the report, its format, or its structure. However, a well-designed rubric or an exemplary lab report would provide the kind of additional information that students need. Arter and McTighe (2001) and Brookhart (2013) recommend presenting students with detailed information on precisely what the teacher wants in an assignment *prior to* students working on it. And this is a commonsense recommendation that we wholeheartedly support.

But another possibility is to use rubrics, exemplars, and detailed notes on strengths and weaknesses *as a form of feedback.* Consider first making the assignment with general information about what is required and then, after students have handed in an initial draft, providing them with more detailed information that they can use to self-assess their work and make revisions before being assigned a grade. This not only will produce a better second draft, but it will also increase students' ability to self-assess and generate high-quality self-feedback—a critical learning skill. As a result, as a teacher you will have less to correct in the second draft; you will be assigning higher grades, and students will be developing important self-assessment skills. Nicol and McCallum (2020) have found this approach to be effective with exemplars. We (Lipnevich et al., 2014; Lipnevich et al., 2022) have found this to be effective with both rubrics and exemplars. In the next section we offer more details on using rubrics and exemplars as feedback.

RUBRICS AND EXTENDED ADVICE

Rubrics have become popular in education and deservedly so. They are simply extended descriptions of what is expected on a given assignment. They are used not only to communicate the assignment to the student, but also to aid in marking and grading the assignment. Rubrics can be very helpful in providing feedback to the student as well.

HOW DID WE GET THE TERM *RUBRIC?*

Although the term *rubric* has become common in education today, few people know the origin of the word. It comes from *rubrication*, which was the practice of writing commentaries and explanations of biblical and other religious texts in red so that they were clearly differentiated from the main text itself. Often rubrications were used to denote the beginning of a new section and to explain what it is about. They were used frequently

(Continued)

(Continued)

in illuminated manuscripts from the Middle Ages, such as the one pictured. *Rubric* actually comes from the same root as *ruby*, meaning red. In the illustration, the first four lines are in red in the original, and are the rubric that explains the passage that follows.

Rubrics were used in religious texts to explain various passages.
Source: The Friedsam Collection, Bequest of Michael Friedsam, 1931.

How does a rubric become a form of feedback? It does so when you have students complete a draft of a project under general instructions, and then provide a rubric that tells them how you are going to mark/grade their assignment. Using the rubric as feedback, students are given a second opportunity to work on their assignment before handing it in for a grade. They can go through the criteria you have set for the assignment and look to see if their work lines up with your expectations. We've conducted research on rubrics (Lipnevich et al., 2014) used on essay assignments and found that students provided with a rubric hand in a second try at an assignment that is significantly better than their initial effort.

Students provided with a rubric hand in a second try at an assignment that is significantly better than their initial effort.

Imagine that you teach biology and your students have just completed a lab report that includes an illustration (dissection of a plant, cells under a microscope, etc.). After they hand in their first drafts, done under a general set of instructions, you provide them with the following rubric and give them a chance to edit and revise their work.

SAMPLE BIOLOGY ASSIGNMENT RUBRIC

Criteria	Outstanding (5)	Well-Executed (4)	Acceptable (3)
Accuracy	Drawings are strong representations of the various components, and labeling is correct.	Drawings are mostly accurate, and various components are correctly labeled.	There are minor errors in drawings, and labels are mostly correct.
Organization	Proportions are correct and labels spaced appropriately.	Proportions are roughly correct and labels readable.	The proportions can be improved, but are not terrible. The labels can be spaced better.
Level of Detail	All levels of detail are seen in the figure.	Level of detail is for the most part very good, but can be improved.	Level of detail can clearly be improved.
General Appearance	The drawing fills a large part of the page while leaving room for labeling, and is clear and easy to make out components and read labels.	The drawing fills most of the space available, and the labels are not cramped but readable.	The drawing does not fill available space but is not too small to see. Labels may be somewhat difficult to read, but not too difficult.

One of your students, Maia, aspires to receive the best possible mark on this assignment and therefore focuses on the "Outstanding" set of criteria, contrasting them with "Well-Executed" to make sure she is on the "Outstanding" side of the ledger. She starts at the top left and checks her drawings. She believes her drawings are strong, and she double-checks her labeling. When she gets down to general appearance, she wonders if her drawings are too small. Her handwriting is exceptionally neat, but very small, and she fears that it might get her marked down. She comes to you and asks for advice. You might say, "I'm sorry, at this point everyone has to make decisions for themselves," or you might say, "It's a little bit small. Think of your reader when you do this. You don't want people to have to work to see the good job that you've done here." In either case, Maia has a decision to make, but only in the second case has she also learned that her handwriting needs to be sufficiently large to be easily viewed and appreciated.

"Yes, but not every student is a Maia."

Providing students with rubrics that have clear descriptions of what is expected of them can have a very positive effect on their performance, and even on their subsequent learning.

No, not every student is a Maia, but research has shown that providing students with rubrics that have clear descriptions of what is expected of them can have a very positive effect on their performance, and even on their subsequent learning.

Quinn (2020) showed that using carefully constructed rubrics with clearly defined evaluation criteria also mitigated racial bias in teachers' scoring, even when there was no evidence of teachers' implicit or explicit racial attitudes. Furthermore, just the chance to work on a project a second time, aided by a clear vision of where the project is headed, can also be of great help. It gives the students a scaffolded opportunity to improve their self-assessment skills. In this case, the scaffolding is the rubric, which explains the goals. In other words, rubrics help with effective self-feedback development.

Closely related to the idea of giving students rubrics is an idea shared with us by one of our colleagues, Ian Tucker (personal communication, January 22, 2020). He collected a set of papers, or exam performances, from a class, and noted students' common problems and misunderstandings. Then he summarized these and handed them out to the next year's class to let them know the typical problems and pitfalls they may encounter. Alerting students to these common errors ahead of time allowed them to become more aware and better prepared to address them.

EXEMPLARS

Exemplars are ideal examples of something. They are a real model for what something or someone should look like. An exemplar should fit the bill of "Here is what a particularly good one would look like."

So imagine any of the following assignments:

1. An essay where the student has a choice of topics

2. A set of math word problems that focuses on estimating the correct answer

3. Drawing an electrical schematic for a doorbell

4. A set of short-answer questions for a history assessment

For any of these assignments, it would be possible to present students with an exemplar from a closely related assignment to show them what excellent performance should look like. Taking a good essay from the same assignment last year would work for assignment 1. A set of math problems worked out with the reasoning provided would be of great help for assignment 2. A schematic for a different kind of problem would work for assignment 3, and a set of questions that aren't going to be used for this assessment would show the students what kind of depth and length are expected in assignment 4.

Similar to rubrics, exemplars can be used as a guide for students working to revise and improve their work. In our research, we have found that students tend to prefer exemplars to rubrics, but we have also found that students actually improve more when using rubrics. This is because the rubric makes them engage more in the underlying issues, while exemplars often give them something to "mimic" without, perhaps, totally understanding why the exemplar represents excellent performance. At the same time, a recent study conducted by one of our students, Ligia Mendonca, with middle school students in Brazil showed that students who received annotated exemplars *after* they produced an initial draft of an essay improved as much as those who received teacher comments (Tomazin, Lipnevich, & Lopera-Oquendo). The difference in time spent on feedback provision in the latter case was 100 times the time spent to choose and annotate an exemplar. Teachers deserve breaks, and exemplars, along with other tools that enhance self-feedback, can save a lot of time while producing a similar outcome.

Exemplars can be used as a guide for students working to revise and improve their work.

A final reminder on exemplars and rubrics: For an assignment or assessment where you are going to allow a "second draft," providing a detailed rubric or exemplar is a good accompaniment to that second chance. If you are thinking of giving students only "one shot" at an assignment, then you probably should hand out any rubric or exemplar along with the assignment. You need to consider what you want your students to be focused on, what your time constraints are, and where your students are in achieving this particular instructional goal.

SUMMARY AND TAKEAWAYS

There are only so many hours in a day and so many days in our lives. Providing feedback on student work is critical to academic growth, but we need to maintain our sanity at the same time. Additionally, we truly want to see our students grow in their ability to critically reflect on and improve their work on their own. We want our students to be able to successfully engage in self-feedback. We need to combine these two desires and look at ways to provide feedback that is highly efficient while maintaining a good level of effectiveness. We also want to increase students' capability to engage in self-feedback. Peer feedback can provide information about current status, if not always ultimate destinations or ways to get there. That benefits both the receiver and the giver of that peer feedback. The giver gets to engage in critically reviewing the same material that they have just completed. So they are engaging in a level of self-feedback, just with somebody else's work.

Electronic feedback can also provide useful information on current status and, with regard to essays, can do a lot of the tedious work of correcting grammar, spelling, and sentence construction errors. Screencasting allows teachers to speak directly to students in an asynchronous fashion. Rubrics and exemplars provide a wealth of information about the desired end state of a performance or piece of work, and can provide the scaffolding that students often need to bring their work to a new level. Admittedly, none of these options are as good as personalized feedback. But all are much, much better than no feedback at all, and can promote much needed self-reflection.

QUESTIONS TO CONSIDER

1. What are the advantages and disadvantages of giving students rubrics and/or exemplars prior to their working on an assignment or after they've handed in a first draft?

2. How could you blend the information from an essay marker program with your own feedback to students?

3. How extensive are the directions you typically give to students on an assignment? Could too much direction hamper creativity or interest level on their part?

4. If you have never used peer feedback before, contemplate how doing so would go over in your class. What benefits could come from this method? What pitfalls might you encounter?

8 EXAMPLES OF INSTRUCTIONAL FEEDBACK

In this chapter, we look at several examples of providing feedback at various levels of instruction. We start with the instructor's goals for using a particular assessment to learn about students and the basis for providing instructional feedback. We then look at a couple of options for doing this, pick one, and walk it through from what a student turns in all the way to the feedback provided. We've deliberately picked a broad range of topics and ordered these by age of the learner.

LEARNING STORIES IN EARLY CHILDHOOD

We begin with the early years and focus on the brilliant work of Margaret Carr and Wendy Lee in their 2012 book, *Learning Stories: Constructing Learner Identities in Early Education*. If you are an early childhood educator, we strongly recommend this book. In this small example, we'll give you some notion of the ideas behind learning stories. But first, a definition and explanation of learning stories, taken from The Education Hub in New Zealand (Hargraves, 2020, bold in original):

> **Assessment in early childhood needs to reflect the complexity of children's learning and development, and the context of their interactions with people, places and things. Less standardised forms of assessment are often the most appropriate for assessing complex learning in context. Qualitative and interpretive methods that focus on showing the learner and their achievements in the contexts of relationships and environments are better able to capture multiple and less pre-determined outcomes.**

Learning stories are narratives created from structured observations, designed to provide a cumulative series of pictures about a child's learning. They are observations that are reinterpreted as stories, then analysed and used as the basis for planning. Teachers collect "critical incidents" or moments which seem significant for a child. By analysing several of these through narrative, teachers can come to understand the path of the child's learning and the pattern of their learning dispositions. Several consecutive narratives can be pieced together to make a fuller picture, while remaining open for other pieces to be added.

The primary audience for learning stories includes parents and extended families, but also other teachers in the school or a child care center and the children themselves. In early childhood educational centers, or preschools, the idea of curriculum is different from that in the upper levels of education, but that is not to say that curricula are not available and used. New Zealand's curriculum for early childhood (called *Te Whāriki*—Māori for "The Woven Mat"), contained at the QR code on this page, is 72 pages long. Again, this is an excellent document and well worth looking at. The learning outcomes in *Te Whāriki* are broader and not tied to strict time frames. Here are two from that curriculum:

https://bit.ly/
3f1yLVY

1. Over time and with guidance and encouragement, children become increasingly capable of enjoying hearing stories and retelling and creating them.

2. Over time and with guidance and encouragement, children become increasingly capable of using a range of strategies for reasoning and problem solving. (Ministry of Education, New Zealand, 2017, p. 27)

Learning stories help teachers, children, parents, and others understand the activities and progress of children and provide ideas for how they might assist in that growth.

Learning stories help teachers, children, parents, and others understand the activities and progress of children and provide ideas for how they might assist in that growth.

Early childhood teachers observe children during the day, take pictures, and carefully note what the children are doing, and then talk about what they have observed. They also think carefully about what is happening and recommend areas for continued growth and development. The following is a learning story for a child named Elodie.

Elodie can do tricky puzzles!

I have noticed Elodie has been really focused when it comes to puzzles lately. She has been attempting trickier puzzles alongside and with her peers. She was able to successfully complete our Matariki* puzzle. This one has proved tricky for lots of tamariki,* but Elodie persisted and used a trial-and-error technique to place the pieces until it was complete. Ka pai,* Elodie! Do you do puzzles at home? We have some large floor puzzles you might enjoy doing with some friends. I will hunt them out for you.

Note: *Matariki* is the Māori word for the Pleiades star cluster (also known as The Seven Sisters, and even Subaru). When it is first seen on the horizon, it is planting season in New Zealand. *Tamariki* is Māori for children, and *ka pai* is "Good for you!"

Elodie's mom responded:

Yes, she loves a 25-piece Minnie and Daisy puzzle we have at home. I should bring out the other 25-piece puzzles we have for her too!

What we see here is the teacher, Alicia Scott, telling Elodie and her parents about what Elodie has been doing at preschool, and very gently suggesting that they might encourage this activity at home. From the picture, we can see that Elodie is clearly pleased with her success.

Thinking About the Feedback

Through her learning story to Elodie's parents, Alicia has provided a good example of a solid approach to feedback. Directly working on a particular skill is not really the curriculum approach here; instead, learning stories are meant to foster the child's interests and inclinations.

Learning stories are meant to foster the child's interests and inclinations.

Alicia begins by telling us what Elodie has been focused on—what *her* goals are (what are the objectives?). Then, she tells us of the success Elodie is experiencing due to her persistence (what does she do?). Finally, Alicia recommends capitalizing on this interest and success by additional, and perhaps more elaborate, tasks (what is next?). Here, Alicia has provided feedback not just at the task level (Elodie was able to complete the puzzle), but also about the strategy she used, moving to the strategy and processes level of feedback here. The feedback also is highly personalized and addresses Elodie directly while speaking to her parents.

WRITING DEVELOPMENT AT THE PRIMARY LEVEL

In the lower elementary years, in Grades K–3, language development is a key part of the curriculum. Reading and writing, and, to a somewhat lesser degree, listening and speaking, occupy a large part of the school day. Teachers are concerned with developing the reading and writing skills of their students and need assessments and feedback in order to reach their instructional goals. In this section we present an example of instructional feedback concerning writing development. It comes from a student who is about three quarters of the way through second grade, and her teacher wants to see where children are in their ability to write a story. The teacher will be looking at how well students have a concept of a story (beginning, middle, end, and perhaps even the resolution of an issue), how they are progressing on grammar and spelling, and how imaginative they are in their stories.

To get a sense of where students are on these issues, she asks them to write a "made up" story. She tells the students to come up with a story like one they would read in a storybook. It can be about anything and should be at least one page long. This assignment gives the students freedom of choice as they can write about anything they like. The teacher hopes that this will engage the students' interest and result in a strong performance. Here is 7-year-old Kaitlin's story based on this assignment.

The mice in the car: Once long ago mice had no home. They went in homes of people everywere. The mice were kicked out. People wanted the mice to get out of town. So the mice did go out of town. The mice was scard of people so they ran. Then 5 mice went into each car that came to a gas stashin. Mice would make a mark on the car so mice wouldn't go in the car if it was marked! Soon every mouse was in a car. So if you hear a rattle or shake thats the mice.

This story tells us a lot! First, Kaitlin clearly has an excellent sense of story. There is a problem, a resolution, and a cute twist/comment at the end. Note that she starts with "Once long ago," suggesting that she has been read a lot of stories and knows their structure. She also says that people wanted the mice to "get out of town," a colloquial phrase. There are a few mistakes, a few misspelled words, and several grammar errors, but they are pretty minor. Furthermore, the misspelled words are difficult words, which shows that Kaitlin is pushing herself to use words even if she isn't certain about the spelling. Feedback here is going to be building on strength.

What does this story tell us about Kaitlin's writing development, and what should we say to her in terms of feedback? To begin, there is not a whole lot to worry about here in terms of correction. We might point out the errors or ask if Kaitlin can spot them, but that is a secondary concern. It might be better to talk about what is good in this essay and how to build on that. We might also inquire about the affective side of this work. Did Kaitlin enjoy writing this? Is this something she likes to do? In second grade, it might be best for feedback to be oral, perhaps a brief one-to-one conversation. The teacher might start as follows:

> *Kaitlin, what a clever story this is! I really enjoyed reading it. We've been working on coming up with creative story ideas, and this is a great example of one. I have to say that I'm pretty afraid of mice, so I would probably have been one of those people telling them to leave. I really like the way you set up a problem with the mice needing a home, and then how they came up with a solution by going into cars. And very clever to show how mice would know if a car was occupied or not. Tell me, how did you get the idea for such a clever story? Did you have other ideas that you decided not to use? (And if so, how did you decide?) Do you enjoy writing stories like this? Have you thought about what might happen next in this story? Or maybe they tried something else first, and it didn't work. There are a couple of spelling errors, but I like to see you trying big words. It's fine if your spelling is wrong occasionally. Keep pushing yourself!*

Thinking About the Feedback

This feedback tells Kaitlin that she is really on the right track and to keep pushing herself. It also makes suggestions for where she could go next if she wanted to work on this story more. In addition, Kaitlin learns that the teacher is fine with occasional small mistakes, and that she should push herself with her vocabulary. Looking at this feedback in terms of our model, we see that it talks about where the class is headed here in terms of being creative (where are we going?), and lets Kaitlin know how she did on this story (how are we going?). It then lays out options for Kaitlin to work on in the future and inquires about her interests in working on stories like this (where to next?). It provides feedback at the task level (feedback overall on the story and on the minor errors), as well as on the processes involved, with the question, "Tell me, how did you get the idea for such a clever story?" It even broaches the notion of self-regulatory behavior by asking Kaitlin if she had other ideas and how she chose this one. It is personal, engaging, and forward-looking.

MULTIPLE-CHOICE READING TESTING IN MIDDLE YEARS/HIGH SCHOOL

Multiple-choice assessments are often used as standardized measures, usually as part of a state-wide assessment program that is high stakes for schools and teachers. Accordingly, they are sometimes looked upon with varying levels of disdain. However, multiple-choice assessments can be useful in providing feedback and in making decisions for next steps in instruction. They are also efficient to give and score promptly, and can be used to communicate levels of performance at the whole-class or individual student level. The major downside is that on a four-choice question, students have a 25% chance of getting the answer correct just by guessing.

Let's imagine that the instructional goal is to continue the development of reading skills for Mr. Berg's eighth-grade class. For some students, this will focus more on nuance and subtleties in a text, and for others it will be getting the facts straight and making minor inferential leaps. Here we can see that there are different goals for different students. Given that this is the beginning of the school year, Mr. Berg would like to get a rough idea of where students are with respect to their reading development so that he can provide the best instruction for the class as a whole, and to help those students with particular areas of need. The following is part of a longer assessment that he has given them. Let's see what we can learn and how feedback might be provided.

Villi Bjorklund sat on the steps in the front of his apartment and wondered where his life had gone. How did he get to be seventy years old, retired, and with his nearest relative three thousand miles away? It wasn't that life was particularly bad for Villi. He had *conscientiously* saved his money all the time he ran his fishing boat. He was almost as big and almost as strong as he was twenty years ago, maybe even thirty years ago. No, it wasn't money or health that was troubling Villi.

He thought about his youth, about growing up in a small village near Oslo, Norway. Of course, that was thousands of miles and fifty years away. He remembered the day that he decided to leave his home and come to America to make his fortune. It was also the day he decided not to marry Olga Knudssen. Those were hard decisions.

On the other hand, had he not made the trip, he wouldn't have met and married Anna Lang, and that would have meant no son in California, nor two fine grandchildren. Now, however, Anna was gone, and Villi wasn't in California. He was in New York City, sitting on his front *stoop*, wondering where his life had gone.

He thought of his younger brother Peer, and how sad he was when Villi said goodbye. Peer had three daughters, two sons, and fourteen grandchildren. Villi had pictures of them all but had never met them. He hadn't even met Marit, Peer's wife.

"What makes a happy child growing up in Norway end up an old man living alone in New York City?" he thought. "Why am I here?"

"Why *am* I here?" he cried aloud, though there was no one to hear.

Villi jumped up, his decision made. He smiled as he climbed the stairs, thinking how surprised Peer would be to see him.

1. Whom had Villi never met?

   a. Olga Knudssen

   b. Anna Lang

   c. Marit Bjorklund

   d. Peer Bjorklund

2. Why did Villi come to America?

   a. To get married

   b. To be closer to his son

   c. To earn a living

   d. To get out of Norway

3. In this story, what does *conscientiously* mean?

   a. Carefully

   b. Hopefully

   c. Sometimes

   d. Intended to

4. What is bothering Villi when the story begins?

   a. He is sick.

   b. He is poor.

   c. He is mourning.

   d. He is lonely.

5. Choose the best title for this story?

   a. "Two Brothers"

   b. "Growing Up in Norway"

   c. "Running a Fishing Boat"

   d. "Villi's Decisions"

Once the scanning machine and program have scored students' responses, Mr. Berg can go over the results. The first thing he notes is that the class seems to have done fairly well overall. On some questions, almost every student chose the correct answer. As a whole, their reading comprehension is fairly strong, at least at a literal level. However, there are a number of questions where the percentage of correct responses drops. The questions with which students struggled most are the inferential questions and the ones concerning vocabulary in context. This is good information for instructional planning. Detective stories, poetry, murder mysteries, and personal reflections are all good sources of developing the ability to make inferences in reading. The problem with vocabulary in context seems a bit more perplexing to Mr. Berg. He looks at the question that the students got wrong on this passage and asks himself, "If I didn't know what *conscientiously* meant, could I figure it out from this context?" He thinks, "All the responses fit to a degree. *Carefully* fits the best, but *Hopefully* is certainly a close second here!" He decides that this idea of figuring out what words mean from context is one that he will bring up for class discussion.

Then he turns to the answers provided on this assessment by a student named Andre. Andre has gotten only about half of the questions right on the whole assessment and has missed all but one of the questions. Mr. Berg decides the best approach to take here is to have a one-on-one chat with Andre about his answers. Their conversation could be as follows:

Mr. Berg:	Hey, Andre, I want to go over this reading test with you so that you can tell me about some of your answers.
Andre:	Sure, Mr. Berg.
Mr. Berg:	I'm really interested in questions 4 and 5. Can you have a look at them and tell me how you chose your answers?
Andre:	Sure. Let me look. OK, on question 4 here, you can tell from the story that he isn't happy. Something has him upset. He's old, but it doesn't say he's sick, and it talks about him saving money, but I wasn't completely sure about that. He isn't lonely because the story talks about all the people he knows, and that's a lot. I don't know what choice C means, so I figured it must be the answer because the other ones weren't right.
Mr. Berg:	OK, good. What about question 5?
Andre:	OK, this one wasn't too hard. First, there's Villi. The whole story is Villi's, right, because he's kind of the guy telling the story. And then there is Peer. His brother. And he talks about how sad he was to leave Peer, and not meeting Peer's wife, and all his kids and stuff. And then the last sentence is about Peer also. So it was easy, right? "Two Brothers." And by the way, Mr. Berg, that giant word there on question 3, no idea!
Mr. Berg:	So did you like this story?
Andre:	Honestly?
Mr. Berg:	Yeah.
Andre:	No.
Mr. Berg:	What kinds of things do you like to read?
Andre:	I'm not too big on reading overall, you know, but I like to read things where stuff actually happens rather than somebody just thinking about stuff. The only thing that happened here is that Villi jumped up. Not too much action, Mr. Berg.
Mr. Berg:	OK, Andre, here's what I'm thinking. This year we're going to be working on getting the most out of your reading—working on what people are implying in addition to what they say directly. This is kind of like when you have to tell your kid brother something you don't want to, so you sort of hint around it. Does that make sense?
Andre:	Yep. That's my kid brother. He doesn't catch on too quickly, though.
Mr. Berg:	Families, huh? OK, good. So as we're working on that, I want you to be right on that, and I think you can be. Now, you missed a number of the questions on this test, but I think maybe it's because these passages weren't of much interest to you. At the same time, you got a bunch right, and I think you basically understood what was going on in these passages. I liked your thinking on both question 4 and question 5. You took both of those

questions on as problems to solve. I appreciate your efforts there. I'd like to see what you can do with some material that you like and maybe where you have more background information. So here's an offer. You tell me what kinds of action stories you like: sports, motor racing, science fiction, superheroes, whatever. I'll find some material that fits what you like, and we'll have another chat about this once you've had a chance to read those. Sound good?

Andre: Sure.

Thinking About the Feedback

A long time ago there was a national television ad campaign with the tagline, "Reading is fun." It later was changed to "Reading is fundamental." We are not sure why it was changed, but we suspect it was because most people don't think reading is fun. No one reads the dictionary for fun. We might read things for pleasure not because the act of reading is pleasurable, but because the content is pleasurable. We also read for business and interpersonal communication. What Mr. Berg correctly sensed about Andre was that he wasn't really fully engaged in the material presented on the test, and that perhaps he would have given the same answers to the questions even if someone had read the material to him. Mr. Berg believed that this assessment had not afforded Andre the chance to show what he could do. So, rather than draw conclusions from it directly, he used it to probe a bit further with what might be called an "assessment interview." That assessment interview showed that (1) Andre didn't really like reading the story, (2) he still put in some good effort, (3) at least some of his answers were based on reasoning even if incorrect, and (4) he would be more engaged if he could read some material that he liked.

Looking at the feedback, it's a bit more complex than what we've seen before because Mr. Berg extended the assessment to gather more information. He then told Andre what the goals were in the long term, where he stood currently, and what they were going to do together to get closer to the goal of stronger inferential reading. His feedback provided correctives, but only in the most general sense, which was probably wise because otherwise, Andre would have had a lot of "this is wrong, and this is wrong," and so on. Mr. Berg then talked about the reasoning strategies Andre had used and noted that they were appropriate for the material. Finally, he provided Andre with an offer to make the year a successful one in his class, which, if tentatively, Andre has accepted. Now, Mr. Berg will have to find those reading materials, but with luck his school is fortunate enough to have a great librarian.

We also have to consider that having a conversation like this with all of his students would eat up a tremendous amount of time, but for many of Mr. Berg's students, it may not really be necessary to have such a conversation. For those who got nearly all the questions right, another time and another assessment may be best for that conversation.

SUMMARY AND TAKEAWAYS

We hope that these examples have presented a way to think about instructional feedback in real settings. As can be seen, it isn't really a "one size fits all" situation. You have to start

Start with your instructional setting, goals, and students, and figure out what you need to know in order to help you help your students progress.

with your instructional setting, goals, and students, and figure out what you need to know in order to help you help your students progress.

The learning stories activity is a really clever way to do this in an early childhood setting. Children at that level typically have a lot of freedom to pursue their interests, and so "catching" them as they are exploring their world is a great way to look at how they are growing and developing. The elementary-level story assignment also offered a lot of freedom of choice for the students in inventing what they would write about. The multiple-choice assessment for secondary students was more "restrictive" and yet offered a lot of useful information, at both the class and the individual student levels. Mr. Berg used the information gathered from the results to its fullest, and then decided that for Andre, and perhaps a few other students, he needed to dig a bit deeper to come up with the appropriate feedback and instructional planning going forward.

QUESTIONS TO CONSIDER

1. If instruction is for the "here and now," how will you develop assessments that provide information geared to the "next steps" that you want to take with your students?

2. For your students, is it better to give feedback less often, but more intensively, or is it better to give small amounts of feedback on a more regular basis? Explain why.

3. What would a one-on-one check-in with a student who did poorly on an assessment look like for you? Write out a sample script for you to follow.

9   FEEDBACK FOR TEACHERS

WHAT FEEDBACK DO TEACHERS FIND MOST USEFUL?[1]

As students filed into the room for their second period Algebra I class, Mr. Rehcaet nervously arranged the papers on his desk. He knew that the school principal, Ms. Foster, would soon arrive for his first classroom observation of the year. Just as he finished, Ms. Foster appeared at the door, computer tablet in hand, and walked to the front of the room to greet him.

Mr. Rehcaet cordially welcomed Ms. Foster, described his focus in the upcoming lesson, and handed her an abbreviated outline that included the lesson's objectives. Ms. Foster thanked him, said that she always looks forward to observing his classes, and made her way to an empty seat at the back of the classroom.

During the class, Ms. Foster took careful notes on how the lesson progressed, the teaching strategies Mr. Rehcaet used, how clearly he explained concepts, and what steps he took to engage students. When the lesson finished and students began their independent practice, Ms. Foster thanked him and the students for allowing her to observe the class and left for her next scheduled observation.

The next day Ms. Foster and Mr. Rehcaet met during his planning period to discuss the observation. She described how well organized she found the class, how clearly Mr. Rehcaet had presented the lesson, and his openness to students' questions. As for improvement, she suggested that Mr. Rehcaet post the learning objectives on the board for students to refer to throughout the class and recommended he try to ask higher-level questions that prompt students to do more complex reasoning. Mr. Rehcaet thanked Ms. Foster for her feedback and returned to his classroom to implement her suggestions.

Does this sound familiar? Can you see yourself in this scenario? Is it similar to most of the classroom observations you've known as a teacher or school leader? We suspect your answers to these questions are "Yes."

But now for the harder questions. Were these types of classroom observations truly helpful to you? Did they guide you in preparing better lessons? Did they offer the feedback you needed to become a more effective teacher and have a more powerful influence on your students' learning? If you're like the vast majority of teachers we know, your answers to these questions are a resounding "No!"

---

[1]This chapter is based on an article coauthored with Dr. Laura J. Link: Guskey, T. R., & Link, L. J. (2022). What teachers really want when it comes to feedback. *Educational Leadership*, *79*(7), 42–48. Dr. Link contributed significantly to that article and developed many of the ideas described in this chapter. Any misinterpretations or misrepresentations, however, are solely our responsibility.

FEEDBACK TO TEACHERS

Teachers today are bombarded with many different forms of feedback. School leaders offer feedback based on classroom observations. Professional learning community colleagues provide guidance on how to improve instructional techniques and boost student engagement. Instructional coaches recommend ways to refine teaching practices and enhance relationships with students. And professional learning sessions present strategies to improve nearly every aspect of the teaching and learning process.

But among all these forms of feedback, what do teachers find most valuable in efforts to enhance their interactions with students and improve their impact on student learning? What information addresses their greatest concerns? What evidence best guides them in becoming better at their craft? When we asked teachers these crucial questions, they were very consistent in their responses. Teachers identified five key characteristics of the feedback they find most useful in improving their effectiveness in diverse classroom contexts (Guskey & Link, 2021, 2022).

1. Teachers Want Feedback on Student Learning

Most teacher feedback, especially what they receive from formal observations by school leaders, focuses on their actions and behaviors while teaching. Leaders note activities such as the following:

- Are the lesson objectives clearly communicated to students?

- Are teachers relying on students' background knowledge to introduce a new concept or skill?

- Is the teacher asking higher-order questions and asking for student feedback during the lesson?

- Is the teacher using techniques to ensure all students participate in class discussions?

Although teachers generally acknowledge the importance of these actions and appreciate knowing when they do them well, most see these behaviors as means to a far more important end: *the impact on students*. In particular, teachers want to know: Do my explanations make sense to students? Are even reluctant students engaged and catching on? Are all students feeling they are part of the class and involved in something meaningful? Occasionally school leaders talk with students during or after an observation and ask these questions, but rarely are they an established component of the formal observation procedures.

The feedback teachers receive isn't what they consider most useful to their professional growth and improvement (Bayler & Ozcan, 2020).

Ironically, school leaders are uniquely positioned to offer this kind of firsthand feedback on student learning. They often know the students, their learning histories, and their family backgrounds. In most cases, they also have some knowledge of the curriculum and learning expectations. But most formal classroom observations occur only a few times each year and are generally disconnected from students' work (Link, 2020). As a result, the feedback teachers receive isn't what they consider most useful to their professional growth and improvement (Bayler & Ozcan, 2020).

Teachers want to know that they make a difference for their students (Lam, 2016). The greatest rewards they derive from teaching come from their impact on students (Walk & Handy, 2018). Most teachers judge their effectiveness not in terms of their teaching actions or behaviors, but rather on seeing how their students think, how they solve problems, and how they feel about themselves as learners (Kraft, 2019). When asked to define "having a good day," they describe seeing their students "get it," observing "the lights go on," noticing "smiles of understanding," and realizing that what they did as teachers made that happen (Guskey & Link, 2022).

2. Teachers Want Feedback From *Their* Students in *Their* Classes

The feedback teachers find most useful is personalized and designed to help them succeed in *their* context. Teachers want ideas that will enhance interactions with the students they see daily in order to gain evidence that shows that they make a difference (Bandura, 2001).

The feedback teachers find most useful is personalized and designed to help them succeed in their context.

Almost all teachers have had the experience of trying new strategies that fail to produce the improvements that were promised. As a result, most teachers become skeptical of innovations that are outside of their personal experiences. Hearing that a strategy worked for another teacher, with different students, in a different school, or in a different state rarely convinces them. Eliminating that skepticism requires personal mastery experiences that offer teachers tangible evidence that the strategy works with *their* students in *their* classrooms (Guskey, 2020).

3. Teachers Want Feedback They Trust

Sources of evidence on student learning vary widely. Measures of student achievement can range from nationally normed standardized tests to results from student projects, classroom quizzes, and formative assessments. Measures of student outcomes can include surveys of students' attitudes, confidence in the classroom, self-efficacy, and social and emotional learning skills. Although debates rage about what evidence is most important, the one thing we know is that school leaders and teachers differ in their perspectives about what evidence is most valid (Guskey, 2007).

School leaders and teachers differ in their perspectives about what evidence is most valid (Guskey, 2007).

School leaders—as well as most school board members, policy makers, and legislators—trust large-scale assessments of student achievement such as standardized tests and state assessments developed by well-established assessment companies. Despite evidence showing that many of these assessments are "instructionally insensitive" (Popham, 2007) and poorly aligned with state curriculum standards (Polikoff et al., 2011), school leaders generally believe they provide trustworthy information about learning progress.

Teachers, however, are more skeptical of standardized testing instruments. Because they are more aware of the misalignment between standardized tests' content and format and the knowledge and skills emphasized in the curriculum, teachers put more trust in the evidence they gather from their students in their classrooms. They trust the results from students' daily work, personal interactions and observations of students,

Because they are more aware of the misalignment between standardized tests' content and format and the knowledge and skills emphasized in the curriculum, teachers put more trust in the evidence they gather from their students in their classrooms.

student presentations and demonstrations, and classroom assessment results (Guskey, 2007).

In a study investigating different types of feedback on students' learning progress, teachers consistently rated tallies of students' errors on classroom formative assessments—that is, ongoing assignments that are not graded—as the most valuable and most useful (Guskey & Link, 2022). Summaries like the one displayed in Figure 9.1 helped teachers identify their instructional strengths as well as areas needing improvement.

FIGURE 9.1 ■ Example of Formative Assessment Error Analysis

**Assessment Analysis
(# of Errors/Item)**

1.	/	11.	///
2.	///	12.	##### ##### ##### //
3.		13.	//
4.	//	14.	#####
5.	////	15.	
6.	/	16.	///
7.	##### ##### ///	17.	##### /
8.	##### ##### #####	18.	//
9.	///	19.	/
10.	//	20.	//

As demonstrated in this figure, most students did fairly well on items 1 through 6, but items 7, 8, and 12 were answered incorrectly by most students. It could be that these items were ambiguously worded or mis-keyed. If so, then the teacher needs to revise them. But if reviewing these items reveals no obvious problems, then the teacher knows these concepts and skills require a different way of teaching. Whatever learning activities or assignments were used, they clearly didn't work for many students. Teachers tell us that this type of feedback is better targeted, more prescriptive, and far more useful than school leaders' comments on their teaching styles.

Teachers need feedback in order to improve their teaching.

4. Teachers Want Feedback Quickly

In some education reform initiatives, improvements in student learning may not be immediately apparent. Sustained support for extended periods of time may be required to achieve the potential benefits (Fullan & Hargreaves, 2013).

Sustained support for extended periods of time may be required to achieve the potential benefits (Fullan & Hargreaves, 2013).

When it comes to classroom-level strategies or procedures, teachers want to see evidence of improvement rather quickly, typically within the first few weeks. If they don't readily see a positive difference for their students, most teachers will abandon the new strategies and revert back to tried and trusted practices. This isn't because teachers are afraid of change or hesitant to try new ideas. Instead, it's because continuing with an untested strategy holds the possibility that their students will learn less well. And most teachers are reluctant to risk their students' learning success for the sake of innovation (Guskey, 2002).

This means we need to establish procedures for teachers to get feedback on the results of their efforts within weeks, not months or years. Results from assignments and classroom assessments provide an excellent source of such evidence. But feedback on improvement in students' daily work, better written assignments, enhanced engagement in class lessons, greater confidence in learning, or improved attendance might prove equally

To implement new strategies, teachers need to know quickly that positive results are not only likely, but also within their reach.

effective. To implement new strategies, teachers need to know quickly that positive results are not only likely, but also within their reach.

5. Teachers Want Feedback Offered in Meaningful, Nonthreatening Ways

Leaders can offer teachers feedback through a variety of formats, including written comments, recorded notes and observations, group discussions, and individual conversations. But regardless of the format, *how* leaders communicate that feedback matters to teachers. Strong evidence shows that if teachers don't receive feedback in meaningful, helpful, and nonthreatening ways, their practices will not change (Cherasaro et al., 2016).

What works best in communicating feedback to teachers closely parallels what we know about offering effective comments to students (see Guskey, 2019). Specifically, effective comments follow a four-step process:

1. Begin with what was positive.

2. Describe what needs improvement.

3. Offer guidance on how to make the improvements.

4. Express confidence in success.

Similarly, teachers appreciate acknowledgment of their successes with students, big or small. This doesn't mean praise but rather simple recognition of their successes. Teachers also want targeted but nonjudgmental feedback on the areas for improvement or where a different approach may prove beneficial. Paired with that feedback, they want specific guidance and practical suggestions on how they might improve. However, they want that advice in the form of ideas and strategies that evidence supports, rather than as mandated practices they are told to use. Instead of "Your instruction needs more student engagement or critical thinking," more effective feedback would sound like "I like the way you incorporated open-ended questions about the text in your lesson, yet some of your students seem more prepared than others to address them. Next time, you may want to employ a short formative assessment before the discussion to check students' individual comprehension levels."

If teachers don't receive feedback in meaningful, helpful, and nonthreatening ways, their practices will not change (Cherasaro et al., 2016).

Teachers want to make a difference, and the feedback that's most useful recognizes that commitment and, in collegial and supportive ways, helps them achieve their mission.

Finally, teachers want to know that their leaders, colleagues, coaches, and advisors believe in them, understand their commitment to students, and have confidence in their success. Ending an example feedback session with "You've got this!" or, more specifically, "I know you'll have all students thinking about what they read in no time" provides the supportive affirmation teachers seek. Teachers want to make a difference, and the feedback that's most useful recognizes that commitment and, in collegial and supportive ways, helps them achieve their mission. Teachers need guidance, and feedback can help them improve.

SUMMARY AND TAKEAWAYS

When it comes to providing teachers with the feedback they find most helpful, what they want and what they most need are the same. Teachers want practical guidance on what they can do to make the greatest positive impact on students' learning. Teachers want to know what they do well, what they may need to revise, and what specific strategies will make their instruction more effective. Trustworthy evidence on student learning gives teachers the information they need to specifically target their improvement efforts and enhance their positive impact on students.

QUESTIONS TO CONSIDER

1. What do you typically expect when you know you are going to be observed?

2. How can you seek feedback that you would like to receive? Can you ask for feedback on teaching, content, or both? Can you ask for advice regarding classroom management?

3. What can school leaders do to deliver meaningful feedback to teachers?

4. If a teacher is struggling with an aspect of teaching (say, feedback delivery), how can you help them to do better? Prepare a script for feedback on various components of teaching.

10 BRINGING IT ALL TOGETHER

Our goal in this chapter is to bring together everything that we've said so far! Without being too prescriptive, we lay out in this chapter the general process we believe should be undertaken for realizing the promise of feedback from the beginning to the end. It is the one reference you can go to in order to check on your efforts or remind yourself of the ideas we've put forward. Our recommended process is as follows:

1. Plan

2. Give

3. Consider

4. Craft

5. Provide

PLAN YOUR ASSESSMENT

Just as you would plan a lesson, a trip, a vacation, a party, or a dinner event, you must plan instructional feedback. The reason here is simple: It will be better if you do. It will allow you to "reflect in advance" on what you want to accomplish and what approach will be the best (strongest, most efficient, most engaging for students, most convenient for your schedule, etc.). At the end of your planning, you should be able to say, "This is what I want to do, and this is how I am going to do it."

Just as you would plan a lesson, a trip, a vacation, a party, or a dinner event, you must plan instructional feedback.

Remember in planning instructional feedback that you don't always have to do it yourself. You may have something that you used in the past that you can simply use again or modify and adapt. You may have heard a colleague talking about an approach they used that would be useful in this situation. You might even find a solid suggestion online or in a book. A wonderful thing about teachers is that they love to share, and the internet has provided the profession with the means to spread our successes widely. Don't be afraid to benefit from the work of others. Nobody ever called someone a great teacher because they were able to generate great ways to gather information for instructional feedback. As we said at the outset of the book, if it isn't your strength, get help!

One issue to consider in planning and developing your assessment is to ensure that the assessment engages your students and allows them to show you what they know and can do. Sometimes a creative video or a poster can be a good approach, depending on the age and background of your students. Just make sure you get to the heart of what you want and are not too influenced by the format.

Ensure that the assessment engages your students and allows them to show you what they know and can do.

USING CLICKERS IN ANIMAL TRAINING

When we want to provide feedback to our students, we can write on an essay, provide a correction and better solution approach in math, or stop a musical or athletic performance and provide feedback. We can even show a student something they did six months ago and comment on it. We can explain in detail just what they did right or wrong, and how to improve.

Imagine you are an animal trainer, or think about trying to train one of your pets. You may be one of those people who like to have long conversations with their animals. But in all honesty, pretty much what they are hearing is "Blah, blah, blah de blah, Daisy." So how do professionals go about training animals?

If you watch shows involving the training and care of animals, you often see clickers used in the training, particularly with dolphins, seals, and other wild animals. The clicker is used as a reinforcement for the animal displaying the appropriate behavior. But how does that work? How does a "click" constitute feedback that rewards animals and lets them know that they have done something correctly? After all, why would an animal like to hear a click?

Kaufman and Pagel (2018) provided the answer to this question. The clicker is called a "secondary reinforcer." First, animals get trained with food as a reward in combination with the clicker. That is, they get trained to associate the clicker with food. Once this is accomplished, the clicker itself is the reward. Of course, you need to combine that with food occasionally to keep the linkage strong. The clicker approach is needed because trainers need to be able to tell the animal exactly when something has been done correctly, and it is often impractical to get food to the animal quickly. But a click in time works just fine.

The process of planning your feedback typically begins with the question, "What do I want to learn about my students so that I can best help them in their learning?" In all likelihood, whatever this is, it is going to be directly related to what you've just been teaching them. But it can also be at the beginning of a lesson where you know little about your students' achievement and want to get a good idea of where to start. The lesson here is simple: Good instructional feedback is based on good information. Good information is thorough, relevant, timely, and accurate.

Good instructional feedback is based on good information. Good information is thorough, relevant, timely, and accurate.

Once you have an idea of what it is you would like to know, the next step in planning is how to create the opportunity for your students to show you where they are. This is sometimes a weak point in the chain of providing powerful instructional feedback and can result in not getting the information you wanted or needed.

Think carefully about what you want to learn about the students, and then devise a task that will allow the students to show you what they can do. For example, math teachers who want to see how students are doing on math word problems would present them with a number of problems to solve and ask them to show their work. They might even ask students to write down difficulties that they are having when working on these problems. The key is to make sure that the assessment is engaging and offers students the opportunity to show you what they can do. This can be done by offering choice in the assessment, but you will need to weigh this against looking at all sorts of different materials from students in developing your feedback. This can be a matter of trial and error.

The nature of the assessment will be closely related to the planning that goes into it. More than anything else, assessments should be "fit for the purpose" and provide you and the student with the evidence needed to determine where the student currently is and where they need to go next.

Assessments should be "fit for the purpose" and provide you and the student with the evidence needed to determine where the student currently is and where they need to go next.

It doesn't have to be complex; it just has to be useful. Sometimes a very brief exercise will work well, and other times you will need something more elaborate.

GIVE FEEDBACK TO YOUR STUDENTS

Obviously, if you are going to provide feedback to students, you need to give them the assessment that you want to base the feedback on. But equally important, you have to consider the conditions under which you administer the assessment so that you can generate feedback.

Consider the conditions under which you administer the assessment so that you can generate feedback.

Probably the first issue you will face is how much time the assessment will take. If it is an "in-class" assessment—a quiz, an essay, and so on—you need to allow ample time for students to complete the assessment, but not so much that many students have to wait on students who need more time to finish. Perhaps you want this to be part of a home-based assignment? Although this can often lead to really excellent and highly informative work, you might not know who was involved in completing the task, or the kinds of resources (or lack of resources) that a child is afforded at home. Some children enjoy a wealth of resources at home while others do not have a place to work or may be in charge of child care, cooking, or after-school employment. This can be a delicate balance to work out.

The next issue is scheduling and consideration of what is going on in your students' lives. Is it wise to assign a major task to be due the Monday after a holiday weekend? Is the school play coming up, or a major sporting event? Are your students receiving major assignments in several of their classes that are due at or near the same time? Students appreciate having their own calendar taken into consideration when teachers decide to schedule assessments.

Students appreciate having their own calendar taken into consideration when teachers decide to schedule assessments.

After checking with your students and other teachers about possible scheduling conflicts, you then need to consider your own calendar. Because the time it takes to grade papers versus grading a quiz is vastly different, you need to take into account your own weekend plans, upcoming travels, and outside commitments when planning turnaround times for feedback. You don't want the efficacy of your feedback to wane because of too long a time lag.

A final consideration is the directions that come with the assignment. Students need to know what they are expected to do and particularly what you are looking for in their work.

Students need to know what they are expected to do and particularly what you are looking for in their work.

Ideal verbal cues include phrases such as "I'm going to focus on how effectively you communicated your ideas about . . . ," "Don't worry too much about . . . ," and "Pay particular attention to . . ." Another way to communicate your expectations is by using rubrics for grading. As we discussed in Chapter 7, providing rubrics to students can be a great help to them in making sure their work is meeting your expectations! Exemplars and summaries of strengths and weaknesses of others who have done this assignment from a previous year can also be a great help.

Ultimately, feedback doesn't have to be based on a formal assessment. It can simply be something you noticed while teaching or watching the students work.

Ultimately, feedback doesn't have to be based on a formal assessment. It can simply be something you noticed while teaching or watching the students work. That is why we refer to it as instructional feedback. As long as you are providing information that is related to student performance, you are delivering feedback.

FEEDBACK: LOVE IT OR HATE IT?

In our research, we have looked at the issue of how people react to feedback (Lipnevich et al., 2016; Lipnevich & Smith, 2009a, 2009b). One question we are interested in is whether some people generally like feedback while others hate it, or whether it is specific to the circumstances and sources of the feedback. The answer to the question is a resounding "Both!"

While it is true that feedback makes some people mostly nervous and others mostly eager, impressions vary depending on the circumstances. On one hand, when you take your car in for its annual mandated roadworthiness checkup, you might be worried that it will fail. On the other hand, when it seems like everything went well in getting a cake into the oven, you cannot wait to see how it comes out! We recently developed and validated a scale that measures students' receptivity to feedback. Here is a link to the technical report containing items as well as scoring guides:

https://osf.io/zt9p8

CAREFULLY CONSIDER
WHAT YOUR STUDENTS TURN IN

A difficult part of instructional feedback is the analysis of the effort that the student has put forth. Teachers need to consider what they're seeing in the work students turn in. What does the paper (video, project, presentation, etc.) tell us about what students can and cannot do, how we can best help them, and what next steps to recommend? Sometimes a poor performance is not an indicator of where the student is in terms of ability or achievement, but rather the effort (or lack of same) in the work turned in. We are reminded of a paper one of our students submitted that was well below the quality of work that was typical of the student. It was a cause for great consternation. How could we break it to the student that this piece of work was pretty close to unacceptable when everything else in the course had been exceptional? After much consideration, it was decided that honesty was the best policy, and a frank but kind review of the work was written. Care was taken to point out exactly where there were deficiencies, and so on. It was returned to the student with some trepidation. The student looked at it and laughed a bit, and then said, "Really sorry about this, Prof. I just got behind in time and knocked this out while waiting for a plane at JFK."

When reviewing student work, in addition to looking at the surface features of the work, you'll want to ask yourself, "What went into producing this response?" "What lies beneath this response?" "What hypotheses can I make about where this student is, and is there any way I can confirm or reject those hypotheses?"

Does an error on a math problem represent the inability to grasp that math concept, was it sloppiness, or an oversight from working too quickly? Are we seeing the student not taking enough time, or not being careful enough in general, in their work? The ability to look for and find root causes often takes years to develop, and it will almost always become more refined with experience. Just like the student with the math problem, when you have students who are experiencing real difficulty, taking a bit more time can be truly helpful.

> When reviewing student work, in addition to looking at the surface features of the work, you'll want to ask yourself, "What went into producing this response?" "What lies beneath this response?" "What hypotheses can I make about where this student is, and is there any way I can confirm or reject those hypotheses?"

CRAFT A RESPONSE

If you are an elementary teacher with a few years of experience, you have probably had a child accidentally call you "Mom" or "Dad." That's because after their parents or family members, you are likely to be the next most significant person in that child's life. So, when you send a feedback message, at any level, it should be a thoughtful message.

That is, it should be thoughtful in the sense of being considerate of the needs of the student, but also mindful of the student's likely response. We have gone over in some detail what all feedback messages should contain, so we will just review them briefly here. First, they should tell the students:

> When you send a feedback message, at any level, it should be a thoughtful message.

1. What are my learning goals?

2. What have I learned?

3. What's next for me?

Feedback messages are most effective if they address not only the level of the task performance, but also the strategies associated with doing the task, and the self-regulatory skills of when to use such strategies.

Ideal feedback messages address all three of these questions. But, feedback messages are most effective if they address not only the level of the task performance, but also the strategies associated with doing the task, and the self-regulatory skills of when to use such strategies. It is not necessary for every message on an assessment to do so. But if the feedback as a whole can do that, the research shows that is what is most effective (Wisnewski et al., 2020).

Feedback should also be timely, be high information (focusing on more than just correctives at the task level), look ahead to the next pieces of work, afford the student the opportunity to improve based on the feedback, and motivate them to do so. Feedback that is personalized and encourages instructional dialogue or conversation is also highly effective.

Feedback that is personalized and encourages instructional dialogue or conversation is also highly effective.

Consider the following sample feedback messages:

- *"Daria, good effort here! Your diagram is almost exactly right. Review your work and see if you can spot an error. It's always a good idea on something like this to start at the beginning and work through your logic all the way before handing it in. I'll look forward to seeing the next version."*

- *"I'm afraid you still haven't gotten this, Jack, but you are so close! Remember that if you do something on one side of the equation, you have to do the same thing on the other side."*

- *"Bend your knees before starting your free throw, Gwen. That will make the whole motion smoother and give you more power. Try it again. Nice and smooth. Watch the ball going just over the rim."*

PROVIDE THE OPPORTUNITY AND MOTIVATION TO RESPOND TO YOUR FEEDBACK

Feedback that isn't processed and acted on by students cannot be effective. Often, feedback is given at the end of an instructional unit, and once it is returned to students, the next unit is introduced. This provides little motivation for the students to review the feedback; especially when they must focus on what's next.

Feedback that isn't processed and acted on by students cannot be effective.

If we want students to absorb the feedback and act on it, there needs to be the opportunity and motivation to do so. A possible strategy would be to allow students to revise their work and hand it in a second time before receiving a grade. It's also possible to build assignments into projects that are going to have an extended life, such as being put on the classroom walls for younger students and being published in a school publication for students of all ages.

Teachers should also consider specific demotivating aspects of feedback. If you are too harsh, students may become frustrated and hopeless and thus reluctant to try. If you are overly enthusiastic, students may lose motivation, thinking they have achieved enough! Be mindful of the basic elements of processing: intense emotions from students will inevitably take up their cognitive resources and result in inferior performance.

We want our students to always know that feedback is their opportunity to improve. The focus is on improvement!

SUMMARY AND TAKEAWAYS

In this chapter we reviewed the process of providing instructional feedback and hopefully showed that it is more of a mindset than a set of steps. Instructional feedback is teaching enhanced by information. It's critical not to lose sight of that teaching benefit; it should be actively pursued. Students need to know when they are successful or have shown areas of growth in an assessment. They also need to know what strategies they can use to improve or correct the errors, and how to determine which strategies are most appropriate for them.

Students need to know when they are successful or have shown areas of growth in an assessment. They also need to know what strategies they can use to improve or correct the errors, and how to determine which strategies are most appropriate for them.

Feedback should focus on underlying processes as well as tasks. Taking this perspective at the planning stage and maintaining it through the entirety of the instructional feedback production, delivery, and follow-up is the best way to maximize its effectiveness.

QUESTIONS TO CONSIDER

1. Think of a time when you received really great feedback. What were the circumstances surrounding that feedback? What were you trying to do? Who provided the feedback? What was its content? Now try this same exercise with feedback that you felt was not helpful to you at all. What can you take from your reflections that you can apply to your teaching?

2. In what situations or activities do you provide the most feedback to your students? How do they typically respond? Are there areas where you could provide more feedback?

3. What resources, assessments, or strategies have you adopted from friends, from fellow teachers, or online? How can you share your knowledge with others around you to promote more effective planning?

4. How will you implement our five-step process—Plan, Give, Consider, Craft, and Provide—in order to realize powerful feedback in your classroom?

REFERENCES

Andrade, H. L., Bennett, R. E., & Cizek, G. J. (Eds.). (2019). *Handbook of formative assessment in the disciplines.* Routledge.

Arter, J. A., & McTighe, J. (2001). *Scoring rubrics in the classroom.* Corwin.

Bailey, J. M., & Guskey, T. R. (2001). *Implementing student-led conferences.* Corwin.

Bandura, A. (1994). Self-efficacy. In V. S. Ramachaudran (Ed.), *Encyclopedia of human behavior* (Vol. 4, pp. 71–81). Academic Press.

Bandura, A. (2001). Social cognitive theory: An agentic perspective. *Annual Review of Psychology, 52*(1), 1–26.

Barnes, M. (2018, January 10). No, students don't need grades. *Education Week.*

Bayler, A., & Ozcan, K. (2020). School principals' instructional feedback to teachers: Teachers' views [Special issue]. *International Journal of Curriculum and Instruction, 12*, 295–312.

Bloom, B. S. (1968). Learning for mastery. *Evaluation Comment* (UCLA-CSIEP), *1*(2), 1–12.

Bloom, B. S. (1971). Mastery learning. In J. H. Block (Ed.), *Mastery learning: Theory and practice* (pp. 47–63). Holt, Rinehart & Winston.

Bloom, B. S. (1974). An introduction to mastery learning theory. In J. H. Block (Ed.), *Schools, society and mastery learning* (pp. 3–14). Holt, Rinehart & Winston.

Brookhart, S. M. (2013). *How to create and use rubrics for formative assessment and grading.* Association for Supervision and Curriculum Development.

Brookhart, S. M., Guskey, T. R., Bowers, A. J., McMillan, J. H., Smith, J. K., Smith, L. F., Stevens, M. T., & Welsh, M. E. (2016). A century of grading research: Meaning and value in the most common educational measure. *Review of Educational Research, 86*(4), 803–848. https://doi.org/10.3102/0034654316672069

Brophy, J. (1981). Teacher praise: A functional analysis. *Review of Educational Research, 51*(1), 5–32. https://doi.org/10.3102/00346543051001005

Brown, P. C., Roediger, H. L., III, & McDaniel, M. A. (2014). *Make it stick: The science of successful learning.* Harvard University Press.

Brummelman, E. (Ed.). (2020). *Psychological perspectives on praise.* Routledge.

Bruner, J. S. (1961). The act of discovery. *Harvard Educational Review, 31*, 21–32.

Burns, E. B., & Frangiosa, D. K. (2021). *Going gradeless, grades 6–12: Shifting the focus to student learning.* Corwin.

Butler, R. (1988). Enhancing and undermining intrinsic motivation: The effects of task-involving and ego-involving evaluation on interest and performance. *British Journal of Educational Psychology, 58*(1), 1–14.

Carr, M., & Lee, W. (2012). *Learning stories: Constructing learner identities in early education.* SAGE.

Cherasaro, T. L., Brodersen, R. M., Reale, M. L., & Yanoski, D. C. (2016). *Teachers' responses to feedback from evaluators: What feedback characteristics matter?* (REL 2017–190). U.S. Department of Education, Institute of Education Sciences, National Center for Education Evaluation and Regional Assistance, Regional Educational Laboratory Central. http://ies.ed.gov/ncee/edlabs

Cooper, H. M. (2007). *The battle over homework: Common ground for administrators, teachers, and parents* (3rd ed.). Corwin.

Cooper, H. M., Robinson, J. C., & Patall, E. A. (2006). Does homework improve academic achievement? A synthesis of research, 1987–2003. *Review of Educational Research, 76*(1), 1–62.

Fullan, M., & Hargreaves, A. (2013). *Teacher development and educational change*. Routledge.

Guskey, T. R. (2000). Grading policies that work against standards . . . and how to fix them. *NASSP Bulletin, 84*(620), 20–29.

Guskey, T. R. (2002). Professional development and teacher change. *Teachers and Teaching: Theory and Practice, 8*(3/4), 381–391.

Guskey, T. R. (2007). Multiple sources of evidence: An analysis of stakeholders' perceptions of various indicators of student learning. *Educational Measurement: Issues and Practice, 26*(1), 19–27.

Guskey, T. R. (2019). Grades versus comments: Research on student feedback. *Phi Delta Kappan, 101*(3), 42–47. https://www.kappanonline.org/grades-versus-comments-research-student-feedback-guskey/

Guskey, T. R. (2020). Flip the script on change: Experience shapes teachers' attitudes and beliefs. *The Learning Professional, 41*(2), 18–22.

Guskey, T. R., & Brookhart, S. M. (Eds.). (2019). *What we know about grading: What works, what doesn't, and what's next?* Association for Supervision and Curriculum Development.

Guskey, T. R., & Link, L. J. (2021, April). *Feedback for teachers: What evidence do teachers find most useful?* [Paper presentation]. American Educational Research Association Annual Meeting, Orlando, FL (Virtual).

Guskey, T. R., & Link, L. J. (2022). Feedback for teachers: What evidence do teachers find most useful? *AASA Journal of Scholarship and Practice, 18*(4), 9–20.

Hargraves, V. (2020, June 4). *How to use learning stories in ECE assessment*. The Education Hub. https://theeducationhub.org.nz/how-to-use-learning-stories-in-ece-assessment-2/

Hattie, J., Crivelli, J., Van Gompel, K., West-Smith, P., & Wike, K. (2021). Feedback that leads to improvement in student essays: Testing the hypothesis that "where to next" feedback is most powerful. *Frontiers in Education, 6*, 645758. https://doi.org/10.3389/feduc.2021.645758

Hattie, J., & Timperley, H. (2007). The power of feedback. *Review of Educational Research, 77*, 81–112. https://doi.org/10.3102/003465430298487

Hussein, M. A., Hassan, H., & Nassef, M. (2019). Automated language essay scoring systems: A literature review. *PeerJ Computer Science, 5*, e208. https://doi.org/10.7717/peerj-cs.20

Kaufman, A. B., & Pagel, M. M. (2018). Instructional feedback in animals. In A. Lipnevich & J. K. Smith (Eds.), *The Cambridge handbook of instructional feedback* (pp. 504–515). Cambridge University Press.

Kohn, A. (1994). Grading: The issue is not how but why. *Educational Leadership, 52*(2), 38–41.

Kohn, A. (1999). *Punished by rewards: The trouble with gold stars, incentive plans, A's, and other bribes*. Houghton Mifflin.

Kraft, M. A. (2019). Teacher effects on complex cognitive skills and social-emotional competencies. *Journal of Human Resources, 54*(1), 1–36.

Kulhavy, R. W. (1977). Feedback in written instruction. *Review of Educational Research, 47*(1), 211–232.

Lam, C. (2016, August 10). 11 rewards of being a teacher. *Edutopia*. https://www.edutopia.org/discussion/11-rewards-being-teacher

Link, L. J. (2020). I explicitly inform teachers/students what successful impact looks like from the outset. In J. Hattie & R. Smith (Eds.), *10 mindframes for leaders: The why, how, and what of the visible learning leader* (pp. 81–89). Corwin.

Link, L. J., & Guskey, T. R. (2019). How traditional grading contributes to student inequities and how to fix it. *Curriculum in Context, 45*(1), 12–19.

Lipnevich, A. A., Berg, D., & Smith, J. K. (2016). Toward a model of student response to feedback. In G. T. L. Brown & L. R. Harris (Eds.), *Handbook of human and social conditions in assessment* (pp. 169–185). Routledge.

Lipnevich, A. A., McCallen, L. N., Miles Pace, K., & Smith, J. K. (2014). Mind the gap! Students' use of exemplars and detailed rubrics as formative assessment. *Instructional Science, 42*(4), 539–559.

Lipnevich, A. A., & Smith, J. K. (2009a). The effects of differential feedback on student examination performance. *Journal of Experimental Psychology: Applied, 15*(4), 319–333.

Lipnevich, A. A., & Smith, J. K. (2009b). "I really need feedback to learn": Students' perspectives on the effectiveness of the differential feedback messages. *Educational Assessment, Evaluation and Accountability, 21*(4), 347–367.

Lipnevich, A. A., & Smith, J. K. (Eds.). (2018). *The Cambridge handbook of instructional feedback.* Cambridge University Press.

Lipnevich, A. A. & Smith, J. K. (2022). Student-feedback interaction model: Revised. *Studies in Educational Evaluation, 75*, 101208. https://doi.org/10.1016/j.stueduc.2022.101208

Ministry of Education, New Zealand. (2017). *Te whāriki: He whāriki mātauranga mōngā mokopuna o Aotearoa: Early childhood curriculum.* https://www.education.govt.nz/assets/Documents/Early-Childhood/ELS-Te-Whariki-Early-Childhood-Curriculum-ENG-Web.pdf

Montessori, M. (2007). *The absorbent mind* (Vol. 1). Montessori-Pierson. (Original work published 1949)

Murray, J., Gasson, N. R., & Smith, J. K. (2018). Toward a taxonomy of written feedback messages. In A. A. Lipnevich, & J. K. Smith (Eds.), *The Cambridge handbook of instructional feedback* (pp. 79–96). Cambridge University Press.

Nicol, D., & McCallum S. (2020). Making internal feedback explicit: Exploiting the multiple comparisons that occur during peer review. *Assessment & Evaluation in Higher Education, 47*(3), 424–443. https://doi.org/10.31234/osf.io/ksp2v

Parr, J. M., & Timperley, H. S. (2010). Feedback to writing, assessment for teaching and learning and student progress. *Studies in Educational Evaluation, 15*(2), 68–86. https://doi.org/10.1016/j.asw.2010.05.004

Polikoff, M. S., Porter, A. C., & Smithson, J. (2011). How well aligned are state assessments of student achievement with state content standards? *American Educational Research Journal, 48*(4), 965–995.

Poorthuis, A. M. G., Juvonen, J., Thomaes, S., Denissen, J. J. A., Orobio de Castro, B., & van Aken, M. A. G. (2015). Do grades shape students' school engagement? The psychological consequences of report card grades at the beginning of secondary school. *Journal of Educational Psychology, 107*(3), 842–854.

Popham, W. J. (2007). Instructional insensitivity of tests: Accountability's dire drawback. *Phi Delta Kappan, 89*(2), 146–150.

Price, D., Smith, J. K., & Berg, D. A. (2017). Personalised feedback and annotated exemplars in the writing classroom: An experimental study in situ. *Assessment Matters, 11*, 122–144.

Pulfrey, C., Buchs, C., & Butera, F. (2011). Why grades engender performance-avoidance goals: The mediating role of autonomous motivation. *Journal of Educational Psychology, 103*(3), 683–700.

Puntambekar, S. (2022). Distributed scaffolding: Scaffolding students in classroom environments. *Educational Psychology Review, 34*(1), 451–472.

Quinn, D. M. (2020). Experimental evidence on teachers' racial bias in student evaluation: The role of grading scales. *Educational Evaluation and Policy Analysis, 42*(3), 375–392. https://doi.org/10.3102/0162373720932188

Sadler, R. (1989). Formative assessment and the design of instructional systems. *Instructional Science, 18*, 119–144.

Scriven, M. (1967). The methodology of evaluation. In R. W. Tyler, R. M. Gagne, & M. Scriven (Eds.), *Perspectives of curriculum evaluation* (pp. 39–83). Rand McNally.

Smith, E., & Gorard, S. (2005). "They don't give us our marks": The role of formative feedback in student progress. *Assessment in Education: Principles, Policy & Practice, 12*(1), 21–38.

Spencer, K. (2017, August 11). A new kind of classroom: No grades, no failing, no hurry. *New York Times.*

Tomazin, L., Lipnevich, A. A., & Lopera-Oquendo, C. (in press). Teacher feedback vs. annotated exemplars: Examining the effects on middle school students' writing performance. *Studies in Educational Evaluation*.

Tyler, R. W. (1949). *Basic principles of curriculum and instruction*. University of Chicago Press.

Walk, M., & Handy, F. (2018). Job crafting as reaction to organizational change. *Journal of Applied Behavioral Science*, *54*(3), 349–370.

Wiggins, G., & McTighe, J. (2004). *The Understanding by Design professional development workbook*. Association for Supervision and Curriculum Development.

Wiggins, G., & McTighe, J. (2007). *Schooling by design: Mission, action, achievement*. Association for Supervision and Curriculum Development.

Wiliam, D. (2018). Feedback: At the heart of—but definitely not all of—formative assessment. In A. A. Lipnevich & J. K. Smith (Eds.), *The Cambridge handbook of instructional feedback* (pp. 3–28). Cambridge University Press. https://doi.org/10.1017/9781316832134.003

Winstone, N., & Carless, D. (2019). *Designing effective feedback processes in higher education: A learning-focused approach*. Routledge.

Wisniewski, B., Zierer, K., & Hattie, J. (2020, January 22). The power of feedback revisited: A meta-analysis of educational feedback research. *Frontiers in Psychology*, *10*, 3087. https://doi.org/10.3389/fpsyg.2019.03087

INDEX

Solutions YOU WANT | Experts YOU TRUST | Results YOU NEED

INSTITUTES

Corwin Institutes provide regional and virtual events where educators collaborate with peers and learn from industry experts. Prepare to be recharged and motivated!

corwin.com/institutes

ON-SITE PROFESSIONAL LEARNING

Corwin on-site PD is delivered through high-energy keynotes, practical workshops, and custom coaching services designed to support knowledge development and implementation.

www.corwin.com/pd

VIRTUAL PROFESSIONAL LEARNING

Our virtual PD combines live expert facilitation with the flexibility of anytime, anywhere professional learning. See the power of intentionally designed virtual PD.

www.corwin.com/virtualworkshops

CORWIN ONLINE

Online learning designed to engage, inform, challenge, and inspire. Our courses offer practical, classroom-focused instruction that will meet your continuing education needs and enhance your practice.

www.corwinonline.com

PLSN209A8

CORWIN

A SAGE Publishing Company

CORWIN HAS ONE MISSION: to enhance education through intentional professional learning.

We build long-term relationships with our authors, educators, clients, and associations who partner with us to develop and continuously improve the best evidence-based practices that establish and support lifelong learning.

Milton Keynes UK
Ingram Content Group UK Ltd.
UKHW051931041123
431953UK00008B/132

9 781544 385211